Legends of
Ancient Egypt

M. A. Murray

DOVER PUBLICATIONS, INC.
Mineola, New York

TO

MY STUDENTS, PAST AND PRESENT,
I DEDICATE THIS BOOK

Published in Canada by General Publishing Company, Ltd., 30 Lesmill Road, Don Mills, Toronto, Ontario.

Bibliographical Note

This Dover edition, first published in 2000, is an unabridged and very slightly altered republication of the work originally published as *Ancient Egyptian Legends* in 1913, by John Murray, London.

Library of Congress Cataloging-in-Publication Data

Murray, Margaret Alice.
    Legends of ancient Egypt / M. A. Murray.
        p. cm.
    Previously published as: Ancient Egyptian legends. London : J. Murray, 1913.
    Includes bibliographical references.
    ISBN 0-486-41137-0
    1. Mythology, Egyptian. 2. Legends—Egypt. I. Murray, Margaret Alice. Ancient Egyptian legends. II. Title.

BL2441.2 .M87 2000
299'.31—dc21

99-054804

Manufactured in the United States of America
Dover Publications, Inc., 31 East 2nd Street, Mineola, N.Y. 11501

Preface

IN this book I have retold the legends of the Gods of ancient Egypt, legends, which were current in the "morning of the world," preserved to the present day engraved on stone and written on papyri. I have told them in my own way, adhering strictly to the story, but arranging the words and phrases according to the English method; retaining, however, as far as possible the expressions and metaphors of the Egyptian. In some cases I have inserted whole sentences in order to make the sense clear; these are in places where the story divides naturally into several parts, as in "The Battles of Horus," and "The Regions of Night and Thick Darkness"; where each incident, so like the one preceding and the one following, is kept distinct in the mind of the reader by this means. This repetition is quite in accordance with the style of Egyptian literature.

The book is intended entirely for the general public, who are increasingly interested in the religion and civilisation of ancient Egypt, but whose only means of obtaining knowledge of that country is apparently through magazine stories in which a mummy is the principal character. It may be worth noting that in these legends of ancient Egypt mummies are not mentioned, except in the Duat, the home of the dead, where one naturally expects to find them.

Though the book is intended for the unscientific reader, I have made some provision for the more serious student, in the Notes at the end. In these I have given the origin of the legend, the book or books in which that original is published, and the book where the translation into a modern language by one of the great scholars of the day can be found. Other translations there are in plenty, which can be seen in specialist libraries; many of these, however, are of use only to a student of Egyptian literature and language.

I have arranged the sequence of the stories according to my own ideas: first, the legends of various, one might almost say miscellaneous, gods; then the legends of Osiris and the deities connected with him; lastly, the legends of Ra. At the very end are Notes on the legends, and a short list of all the gods mentioned.

M. A. M.

November 1912

Contents

The Princess and the Demon

IT was in the reign of King Rameses, son of the Sun, beloved of Amon, king of the gods. A mighty warrior was Rameses; in the day of battle like to Mentu, god of war; very valorous was he, like the son of the Sky-goddess.

Now his Majesty was in Naharaina, where the great river Euphrates rolls down to the sea. And he received the tribute of the vassal-princes, for he was the conqueror of the nine Archer-tribes, and none could stand before his face when he came forth equipped with all his weapons of war. The princes prostrated themselves before him, bowing their foreheads to the ground, breathing the earth which his feet had trodden. Great and splendid was their tribute: gold, and precious stones of all colours, blue lapis lazuli and the green turquoise sacred to Hathor, goddess of love and joy. And slaves came bearing on their backs sweet-scented woods, perfumed and aromatic, like the trees in the land of the Gods.

The prince of Bekhten came also, and with him his eldest daughter; and he placed her in front of the slaves, for she was the choicest part of his tribute. Very beautiful was she, fair in her limbs, tall and slender as a palm-tree, and the heart of the King turned to her with delight, and he loved her more than anything on earth. He made her the Great Royal Wife, and he gave her a name by which she should be known in the land of Egypt; Neferu-Ra, "Beauty of Ra," was she called, for her beauty was like the shining of the sun. And the name was written in the royal oval, as is the custom of the kings of Egypt and their queens.

Then King Rameses returned to Egypt, and with him went the Great Royal Wife, Queen Neferu-Ra. And when they came to the Black Land, the land of Egypt, she performed all the ceremonies of a queen in the temples of Egypt.

Now it happened that King Rameses was in Thebes the Mighty on the twenty-second of the month Payni. And he went into the temple of Amon, for this was the day of the beautiful festival of the god, when the boats go up and down upon the water with torches and lights, and the Sacred Barque, adorned with gold and painted with glorious colours, is borne aloft, that men may see the figure of Amon-Ra himself within. And Queen Neferu-Ra was with his Majesty, for the Great Royal Wife in Egypt has ever been the worshipper of Amon-Ra, king of the gods.

There came into the temple courtiers of the King to announce the arrival of a messenger from the prince of Bekhten. Loaded was he with gifts for Neferu-Ra, Queen of Egypt, daughter of the prince of Bekhten, and he carried also a message to the King. When he entered the royal presence, he bowed to the earth saying, "Glory to thee, O Sun of the nine Archer-tribes! May we live before thee!" Then he bowed to the earth again and spoke the message that he had brought from the prince of Bekhten to Rameses, King of Egypt:

"I come to thee, O living King, my Lord, on account of Bent-reshy, the little sister of the Great Royal Wife, Neferu-Ra; for there is a malady in all her limbs. Send therefore a learned man that he may see and heal her."

The King turned to his courtiers and said, "Bring hither a scribe of the House of Life, and bring also those who speak the hidden things of the Inner Chamber." And the courtiers hastened and brought them into the presence forthwith, and the King said to them, "I have brought you hither to hear this matter. Tell me then of a man, learned and skilful, to send to the prince of Bekhten."

Then they took counsel among themselves as to a learned and skilful man, and they brought the scribe Tehuti-em-heb before the King, and the King bade him go with the messenger of the prince of Bekhten to heal Bent-reshy, the little sister of the Great Royal Wife.

When the scribe Tehuti-em-heb came to Bekhten, he was brought into the presence of Bent-reshy. He was a learned and a skilful man, and he found the princess under the dominion of a spirit, a spirit that was hostile to him, against whom his learning and skill were of no avail, who set his magic arts at naught.

Then the prince of Bekhten was sad, and sorrow was in his heart, but Tehuti-em-heb the scribe counselled him to send again to Egypt and to implore the help of Khonsu, the Expeller of Demons, to cast out the evil spirit from Bent-reshy, the little sister of the Great Royal Wife.

Now so great was the distance from Bekhten to Egypt that from the time that Tehuti-em-heb the scribe departed out of Thebes till the second message came to King Rameses was three years, and throughout that time the evil spirit dwelt in Bent-reshy and would not be cast out.

And when the second messenger arrived, King Rameses was again in Thebes, and it was the first of the month Pakhons, the month that is sacred to Khonsu. He entered into the temple, and with him came his courtiers, and the messenger of the prince of Bekhten. In the temple were two statues of Khonsu; very marvellous figures were these, very sacred, very holy; the one was called Khonsu in Thebes Neferhotep, and the other Khonsu, the Expeller of Demons. Now Khonsu is the God of the Moon, the son of Amon-Ra and of Mut, Lady of Ashru, and men represent him with the curled lock of youth, for he is ever young and beautiful.

Then the King stood before the great statue of Khonsu in Thebes Neferhotep and said, "O my good Lord, I come again into thy presence on account of the daughter of the prince of Bekhten."

Then the priests lifted the statue of Khonsu in Thebes Neferhotep and placed it in front of Khonsu, the Expeller of Demons. And the King spoke again before Khonsu in Thebes Neferhotep and said, "My good Lord, turn thy face to Khonsu, the Expeller of Demons. Grant that he may go to Bekhten."

Khonsu in Thebes Neferhotep inclined his head twice in token of assent. Very marvellous was the figure of Khonsu in Thebes Neferhotep.

And yet again King Rameses spoke, "Let thy protection be with him. Grant that I may send the Majesty of Khonsu to Bekhten to save Bent-reshy, the little sister of the Great Royal Wife."

Khonsu in Thebes Neferhotep inclined his head twice in token of assent. Very marvellous was the figure of Khonsu in Thebes Neferhotep. And he gave his magical protection four times to Khonsu, the Expeller of Demons.

Then King Rameses gave command, and Khonsu, the Expeller of Demons, was placed in the Great Boat; and around the Great Boat were five small boats, with chariots and horses, numerous and splendid, on the right hand and on the left. The retinue of Khonsu, the Expeller of Demons, was the retinue of a king. For a year and five months they journeyed until they reached Bekhten.

The prince of Bekhten came out with his bowmen and his courtiers to meet Khonsu, the Expeller of Demons, with a royal welcome, and they entered into his presence as into the presence of a king. The prince of Bekhten fell on his knees and laid his forehead on the ground at the feet of Khonsu, the Expeller of Demons, and said, "Thou hast come to us. O, be kind to us according to the words of Rameses, King of Egypt."

They brought Khonsu, the Expeller of Demons, to the chamber of Bent-reshy, the little sister of the Great Royal Wife; and he made a magical protection over her. Lo, there happened a wonder and a marvel, for she was well and whole in a moment.

Then the spirit, who had been in her, spoke in the presence of Khonsu, the Expeller of Demons, "Thou hast come in peace, O great God, Expeller of Demons. Bekhten is thy city, its people are thy slaves. I bow before thee, for I also am thy slave. I will go to that place from which I came that thy heart may have peace. But ere I go, let the Majesty of Khonsu give command that a holy day be made for me by the prince of Bekhten."

When he had heard these words, Khonsu, the Expeller of Demons, inclined his head to the priest and said, "Let the prince of Bekhten make a great sacrifice for this spirit."

The prince of Bekhten, and his soldiers and his courtiers heard the voices of the spirit and of the god, and they trembled and were exceedingly afraid. They obeyed the command of the god and prepared a great sacrifice for Khonsu, the Expeller of Demons, and for the spirit that came out of Bent-reshy, the little sister of the Great Royal Wife, the daughter of the prince of Bekhten. And they made a holy day with offerings, sacrifices, and libations.

So the spirit, in the form of a Shining One, went his way in peace out of the land of Bekhten, and he went whithersoever it pleased him, as Khonsu, the Expeller of Demons, had commanded.

The prince of Bekhten was glad and his heart rejoiced, and all the people rejoiced also that the spirit had been driven out of Bent-reshy and out of the land of Bekhten. But in the midst of his joy and gladness, fear came upon the heart of the prince of Bekhten lest the spirit should return and take up his abode again in the land, when Khonsu, the Expeller of Demons, had departed. He took counsel with himself and said, "I will keep Khonsu, the Expeller of Demons, in Bekhten. I will not let him return to Egypt." So Khonsu, the Expeller of Demons, remained three years, four months, and five days in Bekhten, for the prince of Bekhten would not let him go.

And at the end of that time the prince of Bekhten lay upon his bed at night and slept, and while he slept a vision passed before his eyes. He dreamed that he stood before the shrine of Khonsu, the Expeller of Demons; the great doors of the shrine were folded back and the god came forth, stepping out between the doors. He changed into the form of a hawk with feathers of gold, burnished and beautiful, and soared high into the air with wings outspread, and like an arrow he darted towards Egypt.

When the prince of Bekhten awoke, he was exceedingly afraid, for he feared the wrath of the Gods. And he sent for the priest of Khonsu, the Expeller of Demons, and said to him, "The god is estranged from us, he has returned to Egypt. Let his chariot also return to Egypt." The prince of Bekhten gave command that the god should be taken back to Egypt, and he loaded the god with gifts. Great and numerous were the gifts of all manner of beautiful things that the prince of Bekhten gave to Khonsu, the Expeller of Demons.

For many months they journeyed, and with them went an escort of soldiers and horses from the land of Bekhten. They arrived in safety at Thebes, and entered into the temple of Khonsu in Thebes Neferhotep.

Then Khonsu, the Expeller of Demons, gave to Khonsu in Thebes Neferhotep all the gifts, the rich and costly gifts, which he had received from the prince of Bekhten; nothing did he keep for himself. Thus ended the journey of Khonsu, the Expeller of Demons, the great God.

The King's Dream

L ONG, long ago lived Thothmes, King of Egypt; Lord of the Two Lands was he, Wearer of the double Diadem, he whom the Gods loved. He was not that Thothmes, the mighty Bull, who conquered Syria, Nubia, and the nine Archer-tribes. But he bore the same name, and was a great and valorous king; Syria bowed before him, Nubia was his servant, and he trod the nine Archer-tribes beneath his feet. When he was a child, he was like unto Harpocrates, the son of Isis, he who was born in the marshes of the North Country. Beautiful was he with the beauty of the Gods, in form like Horus, the Avenger of his father.

And in all manly sports did he excel; he hunted the wild game on the deserts both north and south of Memphis, he coursed the lions and the deer, he shot arrows at a target, he drove in his chariot, and his horses were fleeter than the wind. Alone did he hunt, or with two companions only, and none knew the path that he would follow, for in the desert none live save wild beasts.

When his followers required rest in the heat of the day, he took them to the great statue of Harmachis close to Kher-aha, where the Road of the God leads eastward to On. Of stone was this mighty figure, hewn out of the living rock, his face the face of a man, stern and majestic, turned to the rising sun, his body the body of a lion; upon his brow is the death-dealing snake with head erect, ready to strike. Men call this figure Harmachis, and the Sphinx, and the Father of Terrors. Great and exalted is this figure of the God, resting in his chosen place; mighty is his

7

power, for the Shadow of the Sun is upon him. The temples of Memphis and the temples of every town on both sides adore him, they stretch out their hands to him in adoration, sacrifices and libations are made before him.

One day, ere Thothmes was yet king, before he had ascended the throne of Horus the Living One, it came to pass that he hunted alone in the desert, and it was noontide. Very fierce was the heat, very blinding the sunbeams, and he rested in the shadow of the great God. And as he rested, heated and weary, in the coolness of the shadow, sleep heavy and deep came upon him at the moment when the sun reached the zenith.

Thus he slept at broad midday, and in his sleep dreams and visions came to him. In his dream he stood before the giant figure of the God, but no longer was it of stone, for behold it was the God himself. The breath of life was in him, and his lips moved, and he spoke with gentle speech as a father speaks with his child, for his words were words of blessing.

"See now, O my son Thothmes," he said, "look at me, behold me. I am thy father, I who am Harmachis, and Ra, and Khepera, and Atmu also. For I am the Sun-god to whom all lands are subject. Through me alone shall the kingdom of Egypt come to thee; thou shalt wear the White Crown of the South Land and the Red Crown of the North Land, thou shalt sit upon the throne of Geb the inheritor. To thee shall belong the whole land in its length and breadth, that land which the universal Lord makes glorious. Want and trouble shall never come nigh thee, for gifts shall be brought to thee from every country, near and afar; the duration of thy life shall be for many years; my face shall be towards thee and my heart shall incline to thee if thou wilt do for me that which I desire of thee."

And Thothmes looked, and he saw that the figure lay half-buried in the sand, and it seemed as though the God struggled to free himself, for naught but the head appeared above the plain, and the sands came up about him like the waves of the sea when they swallow up a ship that is on the rocks.

Then the Majesty of the God spoke again, and said, "The sand of the desert on which I rest is about me, it overwhelms me, it covers me. Hasten to do that which my heart desires, for I know that thou art a son who honours the behests of his father."

Sleep fell from the eyelids of Thothmes, and he awoke.

[Here the inscription is broken away and the end of the story is not known.]

The Coming of the Great Queen

Now Amon-Ra, king of the gods, sat upon his throne, and around him stood the greatest of the gods and goddesses. On his right was Osiris crowned with the great White Crown of the South Land; on his left was Mentu, god of war, and on the head of Mentu were two great feathers and the flashing disk of the sun. With Osiris were the twin goddesses Isis and Nephthys, beside them stood Hathor, goddess of love, whom the Greeks call Aphrodite; Horus, the son of Isis, with the far-seeing eyes of the hawk; and Anubis, son of Nephthys, the faithful guardian of Isis. With Mentu were Atmu, the god of the sunset; Shu and his twin-sister Tefnut; Geb the earth-god, and Nut the sky-goddess. These two are the oldest of the gods, from whom all others proceed.

Amon-Ra, king of the gods, sat upon his throne and looked upon the land of Egypt, and he spoke, saying, "I will create a queen to rule over Tamery, I will unite the Two Lands in peace for her, and in her hands I will place the whole world. Egypt and Syria, Nubia and Punt, the land of the Gods, shall be under her sway." And when he had spoken there was silence among the gods.

While he yet spoke, Thoth entered into his presence, Thoth, the twice-great, the maker of magic, the lord of Khemennu. He listened to the words of Amon-Ra, king of the gods, and in the silence that followed he spoke:

"O Amon-Ra, Lord of the thrones of the Two Lands, King of the gods, Maker of men. Behold in the Black Land in the palace of the king is a maiden, fair and beautiful is she in all her limbs.

10

Aahmes is her name, and she is wife to the king of Egypt. She alone can be the mother of the great Queen, whom thou wilt create to rule over the Two Lands. She is in the palace of the king. Come, let us go to her."

Now the form of Thoth is the form of an ibis, that he may fly swiftly through the air and none may know him, and as an ibis he went to the palace of the king. But Amon-Ra took upon himself the shape of the king of Egypt. Great was the majesty of Amon-Ra, splendid his adornments. On his neck was the glittering collar of gold and precious stones, on his arms were bracelets of pure gold and electrum, and on his head were two plumes; by the plumes alone could men know the King of the gods. In one hand he carried the sceptre of power, in the other the emblem of life. Glorious was he as the sun at midday, and the perfumes of the land of Punt were around him.

In the palace of the king of Egypt was queen Aahmes, and it was night. She lay upon her couch, and sleep was upon her eyelids. Like a jewel was she in her beauty, and the chamber in which she slept was like the setting of the jewel; black bronze and electrum, acacia wood and ebony, were the adornments of the palace, and her couch was in the form of a fierce lion.

Through the two Great Doors of the palace went the gods; none saw them, none beheld them. And with them came Neith, goddess of Sais, and Selk the scorpion goddess. On the head of Neith were the shield and crossed arrows; on the head of Selk a scorpion bearing in each claw the emblem of life.

The fragrance of the perfumes of Punt filled the chamber, and queen Aahmes awoke and beheld Amon-Ra, King of the gods, Maker of men. In majesty and beauty he appeared before her, and her heart was filled with joy. He held towards her the sign of life, and in her hand he laid the sign of life and the sceptre of power. And Neith and Selk lifted the couch on which the queen reposed and held it high in the air, that she might be raised above the ground, on which mortal men live, while she spoke with the immortal Gods.

Then Amon-Ra returned and was enthroned among the Gods. And he summoned to his presence Khnum the creator, he who fashions the bodies of men, who dwells beside the rushing waters of the cataract. To Khnum he gave command saying, "O Khnum, fashioner of the bodies of men, fashion for me my daughter, she who shall be the great Queen of Egypt. For I will give to her all life and satisfaction, all stability and all joy of heart for ever."

Khnum the creator, the fashioner of the bodies of men, the dweller by the cataract, made answer to Amon-Ra, "I will form for thee thy daughter, and her form shall be more glorious than the Gods, for the greatness of her dignity as King of the South and North."

Then he brought his potter's wheel, and took clay, and with his hands he fashioned the body of the daughter of queen Aahmes and the body of her *ka*. And the body of the child and the body of the *ka* were alike in their limbs and their faces, and none but the Gods could know them apart. Beautiful were they with the beauty of Amon-Ra, more glorious were they than the Gods.

Beside the potter's wheel knelt Hekt, lady of Herur, goddess of birth. In each hand she held the sign of life, and as the wheel turned and the bodies were fashioned, she held it towards them that life might enter into the lifeless clay.

Then Khnum, the fashioner of the bodies of men, and Hekt the goddess of birth, came to the palace of the king of Egypt; and with them came Isis, the great Mother, and her sister Nephthys; Meskhent also and Ta-urt, and Bes the protector of children. The spirits of Pé and the spirits of Dep came with them to greet the daughter of Amon-Ra and of queen Aahmes.

And when the child appeared, the goddesses rejoiced, and the spirits of Pé and the spirits of Dep chanted praises to her honour, for the daughter of Amon-Ra was to sit upon the throne of Horus of the Living, and rule the Land of Egypt to the glory of the Gods. Hatshepsut was she called, Chief of Noble Women, divine of Diadems, favourite of the Goddesses, beloved of Amon-Ra. And to her the Gods granted that she should be mistress of all lands within the circuit of the sun, and that she should appear as king upon the throne of Horus before the glories of the Great House. And upon her was the favour of Amon-Ra for ever.

The Book of Thoth

Now Ahura was the wife of Nefer-ka-ptah, and their child was Merab; this was the name by which he was registered by the scribes in the House of Life. And Nefer-ka-ptah, though he was the son of the King, cared for naught on earth but to read the ancient records, written on papyrus in the House of Life or engraved on stone in the temples; all day and every day he studied the writings of the ancestors.

One day he went into the temple to pray to the Gods, but when he saw the inscriptions on the walls he began to read them; and he forgot to pray, he forgot the Gods, he forgot the priests, he forgot all that was around him until he heard laughter behind him. He looked round and a priest stood there, and from him came the laughter.

"Why laughest thou at me?" said Nefer-ka-ptah.

"Because thou readest these worthless writings," answered the priest. "If thou wouldest read writings that are worth the reading I can tell thee where the Book of Thoth lies hidden."

Then Nefer-ka-ptah was eager in his questions, and the priest replied, "Thoth wrote the Book with his own hand, and in it is all the magic in the world. If thou readest the first page, thou wilt enchant the sky, the earth, the abyss, the mountains, and the sea; thou wilt understand the language of the birds of the air, and thou wilt know what the creeping things of earth are saying, and thou wilt see the fishes from the darkest depths of the sea. And if thou readest the other page, even though thou wert dead and in the world of ghosts, thou couldest come back to earth in the form thou once hadst. And besides this, thou wilt see the

13

sun shining in the sky with the full moon and the stars, and thou wilt behold the great shapes of the Gods."

Then said Nefer-ka-ptah, "By the life of Pharaoh, that Book shall be mine. Tell me whatsoever it is that thou desirest, and I will do it for thee."

"Provide for my funeral," said the priest. "See that I am buried as a rich man, with priests and mourning women, offerings, libations, and incense. Then shall my soul rest in peace in the Fields of Aalu. One hundred pieces of silver must be spent upon my burying."

Then Nefer-ka-ptah sent a fleet messenger to fetch the money, and he paid one hundred pieces of silver into the priest's hands. When the priest had taken the silver, he said to Nefer-ka-ptah:

> "The Book is at Koptos in the middle of the river.
> In the middle of the river is an iron box,
> In the iron box is a bronze box,
> In the bronze box is a keté-wood box,
> In the keté-wood box is an ivory-and-ebony box,
> In the ivory-and-ebony box is a silver box,
> In the silver box is a gold box,
> And in the gold box is the Book of Thoth.
> Round about the great iron box are snakes and scorpions and all manner of crawling things, and above all there is a snake which no man can kill. These are set to guard the Book of Thoth."

When the priest had finished speaking, Nefer-ka-ptah ran out of the temple, for his joy was so great that he knew not where he was. He ran quickly to find Ahura to tell her about the Book and that he would go to Koptos and find it.

But Ahura was very sorrowful, and said, "Go not on this journey, for trouble and grief await thee in the Southern Land."

She laid her hand upon Nefer-ka-ptah as though she would hold him back from the sorrow that awaited him. But he would not be restrained, and broke away from her and went to the King his father.

He told the King all that he had learned, and said, "Give me the royal barge, O my father, that I may go to the Southern Land with my wife Ahura and my son Merab. For the Book of Thoth I must and will have."

So the King gave orders and the royal barge was prepared, and in it Nefer-ka-ptah, Ahura, and Merab sailed up the river to the Southern Land as far as Koptos. When they arrived at Koptos, the high priest and all the priests of Isis of Koptos came down to the river to welcome Nefer-ka-ptah, Ahura, and Merab. And they went in a great procession to the temple of the Goddess, and Nefer-ka-ptah sacrificed an ox and a goose and poured a libation of wine to Isis of Koptos and her son Harpocrates. After this, the priests of Isis and their wives made a great feast for four days in honour of Nefer-ka-ptah and Ahura.

On the morning of the fifth day, Nefer-ka-ptah called to him a priest of Isis, a great magician learned in all the mysteries of the Gods. And together they made a little magic box, like the cabin of a boat, and they made men and a great store of tackle, and put the men and the tackle in the magic cabin. Then they uttered a spell over the cabin, and the men breathed and were alive, and began to use the tackle. And Nefer-ka-ptah sank the magic cabin in the river, saying, "Workmen, workmen! Work for me!" And he filled the royal barge with sand and sailed away alone, while Ahura sat on the bank of the river at Koptos, and watched and waited, for she knew that sorrow must come of this journey to the Southern Land.

The magic men in the magic cabin toiled all night and all day for three nights and three days along the bottom of the river; and when they stopped the royal barge stopped also, and Nefer-ka-ptah knew that he had arrived where the Book lay hidden.

He took the sand out of the royal barge and threw it into the water, and it made a gap in the river, a gap of a schoenus long and a schoenus wide; in the middle of the gap lay the iron box, and beside the box was coiled the great snake that no man can kill, and all around the box on every side to the edge of the walls of water were snakes and scorpions and all manner of crawling things.

Then Nefer-ka-ptah stood up in the royal barge, and across the water he cried to the snakes and scorpions and crawling things; a loud and terrible cry, and the words were words of magic. As soon as his voice was still, the snakes and scorpions and crawling things were still also, for they were enchanted by means of the magic words of Nefer-ka-ptah, and they could not move. Nefer-ka-ptah brought the royal barge to the edge of the

gap, and he walked through the snakes and scorpions and crawling things, and they looked at him, but could not move because
of the spell that was on them.

And now Nefer-ka-ptah was face to face with the snake that
no man could kill, and it reared itself up ready for battle. Nefer-
ka-ptah rushed upon it and cut off its head, and at once the head
and body came together, each to each, and the snake that no
man could kill was alive again, and ready for the fray. Again
Nefer-ka-ptah rushed upon it, and so hard did he strike that the
head was flung far from the body, but at once the head and body
came together again, each to each, and again the snake that no
man could kill was alive and ready to fight. Then Nefer-ka-ptah
saw that the snake was immortal and could not be slain, but
must be overcome by subtle means. Again he rushed upon it
and cut it in two, and very quickly he put sand on each part, so
that when the head and body came together there was sand
between them and they could not join, and the snake that no
man could kill lay helpless before him.

Then Nefer-ka-ptah went to the great box where it stood in
the gap in the middle of the river, and the snakes and scorpions
and crawling things watched, but they could not stop him.

He opened the iron box and found a bronze box,
He opened the bronze box and found a keté-wood box,
He opened the keté-wood box and found an ivory-and-ebony box,
He opened the ivory-and-ebony box and found a silver box,
He opened the silver box and found a gold box,
He opened the gold box and found the Book of Thoth.

He opened the Book and read a page, and at once he had
enchanted the sky, the earth, the abyss, the mountains, and the
sea, and he understood the language of birds, fish, and beasts.
He read the second page and he saw the sun shining in the sky,
with the full moon and the stars, and he saw the great shapes of
the Gods themselves; and so strong was the magic that the fishes came up from the darkest depths of the sea. So he knew that
what the priest had told him was true.

Then he thought of Ahura waiting for him at Koptos, and he
cast a magic spell upon the men that he had made, saying

"Workmen, workmen! Work for me! and take me back to the place from which I came." They toiled day and night till they came to Koptos, and there was Ahura sitting by the river, having eaten nothing and drunk nothing since Nefer-ka-ptah went away. For she sat waiting and watching for the sorrow that was to come upon them.

But when she saw Nefer-ka-ptah returning in the royal barge, her heart was glad and she rejoiced exceedingly. Nefer-ka-ptah came to her and put the Book of Thoth into her hands and bade her read it. When she read the first page, she enchanted the sky, the earth, the abyss, the mountains, and the sea, and she understood the language of birds, fish, and beasts; and when she read the second page, she saw the sun shining in the sky, with the full moon and the stars, and she saw the great shapes of the Gods themselves; and so strong was the magic that the fishes came up from the darkest depths of the sea.

Nefer-ka-ptah now called for a piece of new papyrus and for a cup of beer; and on the papyrus he wrote all the spells that were in the Book of Thoth. Then he took the cup of beer and washed the papyrus in the beer, so that all the ink was washed off and the papyrus became as though it had never been written on. And Nefer-ka-ptah drank the beer, and at once he knew all the spells that had been written on the papyrus, for this is the method of the great magicians.

Then Nefer-ka-ptah and Ahura went to the temple of Isis and gave offerings to Isis and Harpocrates, and made a great feast, and the next day they went on board the royal barge and sailed joyfully away down the river towards the Northern Land.

But behold, Thoth had discovered the loss of his Book, and Thoth raged like a panther of the South, and he hastened before Ra and told him all, saying, "Nefer-ka-ptah has found my magic box and opened it, and has stolen my Book, even the Book of Thoth; he slew the guards that surrounded it, and the snake that no man can kill lay helpless before him. Avenge me, O Ra, upon Nefer-ka-ptah, son of the King of Egypt."

The Majesty of Ra answered and said, "Take him and his wife and his child, and do with them as thou wilt." And now the sorrow for which Ahura watched and waited was about to come

upon them, for Thoth took with him a Power from Ra to give
him his desire upon the stealer of his Book.

As the royal barge sailed smoothly down the river, the little
boy Merab ran out from the shade of the awning and leaned
over the side watching the water. And the Power of Ra drew
him, so that he fell into the river and was drowned. When he
fell, all the sailors on the royal barge and all the people walking
on the river-bank raised a great cry, but they could not save him.
Nefer-ka-ptah came out of the cabin and read a magical spell
over the water, and the body of Merab came to the surface and
they brought it on board the royal barge. Then Nefer-ka-ptah
read another spell, and so great was its power that the dead
child spoke and told Nefer-ka-ptah all that had happened
among the Gods, that Thoth was seeking vengeance, and that
Ra had granted him his desire upon the stealer of his Book.

Nefer-ka-ptah gave command, and the royal barge returned
to Koptos, that Merab might be buried there with the honour
due to the son of a prince. When the funeral ceremonies were
over, the royal barge sailed down the river towards the Northern
Land. A joyful journey was it no longer, for Merab was dead, and
Ahura's heart was heavy on account of the sorrow that was still
to come, for the vengeance of Thoth was not yet fulfilled.

They reached the place where Merab had fallen into the
water, and Ahura came out from under the shade of the awning,
and she leaned over the side of the barge, and the Power of Ra
drew her so that she fell into the river and was drowned. When
she fell, all the sailors in the royal barge and all the people walking on the river-bank raised a great cry, but they could not save
her. Nefer-ka-ptah came out of the cabin and read a magical
spell over the water, and the body of Ahura came to the surface,
and they brought it on board the royal barge. Then Nefer-ka-
ptah read another spell, and so great was its power that the dead
woman spoke and told Nefer-ka-ptah all that had happened
among the Gods, that Thoth was still seeking vengeance, and
that Ra had granted him his desire upon the stealer of his Book.

Nefer-ka-ptah gave command and the royal barge returned to
Koptos, that Ahura might be buried there with the honour due
to the daughter of a king. When the funeral ceremonies were

over, the royal barge sailed down the river towards the Northern Land. A sorrowful journey was it now, for Ahura and Merab were dead, and the vengeance of Thoth was not yet fulfilled.

They reached the place where Ahura and Merab had fallen into the water, and Nefer-ka-ptah felt the Power of Ra drawing him. Though he struggled against it he knew that it would conquer him. He took a piece of royal linen, fine and strong, and made it into a girdle, and with it he bound the Book of Thoth firmly to his breast, for he was resolved that Thoth should never have his Book again.

Then the Power drew him yet more strongly, and he came from under the shade of the awning and threw himself into the river and was drowned. When he fell, all the sailors of the royal barge and all the people walking on the river-bank raised a great cry, but they could not save him. And when they looked for his body they could not find it. So the royal barge sailed down the river till they reached the Northern Land and came to Memphis, and the chiefs of the royal barge went to the King and told him all that had happened.

The King put on mourning raiment; he and his courtiers, the high priest and all the priests of Memphis, the King's army and the King's household, were clothed in mourning apparel, and they walked in procession to the haven of Memphis to the royal barge. When they came to the haven, they saw the body of Nefer-ka-ptah floating in the water beside the barge, close to the great steering-oars. And this marvel came to pass because of the magical powers of Nefer-ka-ptah; even in death he was a great magician by reason of the spells he had washed off the papyrus and drunk in the beer.

Then they drew him out of the water, and they saw the Book of Thoth bound to his breast with the girdle of royal linen. And the King gave command that they should bury Nefer-ka-ptah with the honour due to the son of a king, and that the Book of Thoth should be buried with him.

Thus was the vengeance of Thoth fulfilled, but the Book remained with Nefer-ka-ptah.

Osiris

IN the beginning Ra cursed Nut, and his curse was that none of her children should be born on any day of any year. And Nut cried to Thoth who loved her, Thoth, the twice great, god of magic and learning and wisdom, he whom the Greeks called Hermes Trismegistos. Though the curse of the great God Ra once uttered could never be recalled, Thoth by his wisdom opened a way of escape. He went to the Moon-god, whose brightness was almost equal to that of the Sun itself, and challenged him to a game of dice. Great were the stakes on either side, but the Moon's were the greatest, for he wagered his own light. Game after game they played and always the luck was with Thoth, till the Moon would play no more. Then Thoth, the twice great, gathered up the light he had won, and by his power and might he formed it into five days. And since that time the Moon has not had light enough to shine throughout the month; but dwindles away into darkness, and then comes slowly to his full glory; for the light of five whole days was taken from him. And these five days Thoth placed between the end of the old year and the beginning of the new year, keeping them distinct from both; and on these five days the five children of Nut were born; Osiris on the first day, Horus on the second, Set on the third, Isis on the fourth, and Nephthys on the fifth. Thus the curse of Ra was both fulfilled and made of no effect, for the days on which the children of Nut were born belonged to no year.

When Osiris was born, wonders and marvels, prodigies and signs, were heard and seen throughout the world, for a voice cried over the whole earth, "The Lord of all comes forth to the light." And a woman drawing water from the holy place of the temple was filled with the divine afflatus and rushed forth crying, "Osiris the King is born."

Now Egypt was a barbarous country where men fought together and ate human flesh; naught did they know of the gods, lawless were they and savage. But Osiris became the King of Egypt, and he showed his people how to till the land and to plant corn and the vine, and he taught them the honour due to the Gods, and made laws, and abolished their barbarous and savage customs. Wherever he went, the people bowed at his feet, for they loved the very ground he trod on; and whatever he commanded, that they did. Thus did Osiris rule over the Egyptians till, with music playing and banners flying, he passed out of Egypt to bring all nations beneath his gracious sway.

But Set hated his brother Osiris, and he gathered to himself seventy-two conspirators, and with them was Aso, queen of Ethiopia. And they made a plan that when Osiris returned they should kill him and place Set on the throne; but they hid their plans, and with smiling faces went out to meet Osiris when he re-entered Egypt in triumph.

In secret they met again and again, in secret also they prepared a coffer made of costly wood painted and decorated with rich designs and glowing colours, an interweaving of tints and a wealth of cunning workmanship, so that all who saw it longed to have it for their own. Set, that Wicked One, had in secret measured the body of Osiris, and the coffer was made to fit the body of the King, for this was part of the plan.

When all was ready, Set bade his brother and the seventy-two conspirators to a feast in his great banqueting-hall. When the feast was over, they sang the chant of Maneros, as was the custom, and slaves carried round cups of wine and threw garlands of flowers round the necks of the guests, and poured perfume upon them, till the hall was filled with sweet odours. And while their hearts were glad, slaves entered bearing the coffer, and all the guests cried out at the sight of its beauty.

Then Set stood up in his place and said, "He who lies down in this coffer and whom it fits, to that man I will give it." His words were sweet as honey, but in his heart was the bitterness of evil.

One after one, the conspirators lay down in the coffer with jests and laughter; for one it was too long, and for another it was too short, and for a third it was too wide, and for a fourth too narrow. Then came Osiris to take his turn, and he, all unsuspecting, lay down in it. At once the conspirators seized the lid and clapped it on; some nailed it firmly in its place, while others poured molten lead into all the openings lest he should breathe and live. Thus died the great Osiris, he who is called Unnefer the Triumphant, and by his death he entered into the Duat, and became King of the Dead and Ruler of those who are in the West.

The conspirators lifted the chest, which was now a coffin, and carried it to the river-bank. They flung it far into the water, and Hapi the Nile-god caught it and carried it upon his stream to the sea; the Great Green Waters received it and the waves bore it to Byblos and lifted it into a tamarisk-tree that grew by the shore. Then the tree shot forth great branches and put out leaves and flowers to make a fit resting-place for the God, and the fame of its beauty went throughout the land.

In Byblos ruled King Malkander and his wife, Queen Athenais. They came to the sea-shore to gaze upon the tree, for naught could be seen but leaves and blossoms which hid the coffin from all eyes. Then King Malkander gave command and the tree was cut down and carried to the royal palace to make a pillar therein, for it was worthy to be used in a king's house. All men wondered at its beauty, though none knew that it held the body of a God.

Now Isis feared Set exceedingly. His smooth words did not deceive her, and she knew of his enmity to Osiris, but the great King would not believe in his brother's wickedness. When the soul of Osiris passed from his body, at once Isis was aware that he was dead, though no man told her. She took her little son, whom men call Harpocrates or Horus the Child, and fled with him to the marshes of the Delta, and hid him in the city of Pé. Ancient and gray was this city of Pé and it stood on an island; there dwelt the goddess Uazet, whom men call also Buto and Latona, for she is worshipped under many names. Uazet took the child and sheltered him, and Isis by her divine power loosed the island from its moorings, and it floated on the surface of the Great Green Waters, so that no man could tell where to find it. For she feared the power of Set lest he should destroy the child as he had destroyed the father.

As the souls of men cannot rest until the funeral rites are performed and the funeral sacrifices offered, she journeyed, solitary and alone, to seek the body of her husband, and bury it as became his greatness. Many people did she meet, both men and women, but none had seen the chest, and in this matter her power was of no avail. Then she thought to ask the children, and at once they told her of a painted coffer floating on the Nile. And to this day children have prophetic power and can declare the will of the Gods and the things that are yet for to come.

Thus, asking always of the children, Isis came to Byblos. She sat by the Great Green Waters, and the maidens of Queen Athenais came to bathe and disport themselves in the waves. Then Isis spoke to them and braided their hair and adjusted their jewels; the breath of the Goddess was sweeter than the odours of the Land of Punt, and it perfumed the hair and the jewels and the garments of the maidens. When they returned to the palace, Queen Athenais asked them whence they had obtained the perfume, and they answered, "A woman, strange and sad, sat by the sea-shore when we went to bathe, and she braided our hair and adjusted our jewels, and from her came the perfume, though we know not how." Queen Athenais went to the shore to see the strange woman and conversed with her, and they spoke together as mothers speak, for each had a little son; the son of Isis was far away and the son of Athenais was sick unto death.

Then rose up Isis, the Mighty in Magic, the skilful Healer, and said, "Bring me to your son!" Together the Goddess and the Queen returned to the palace, and Isis took little Diktys in her arms and said, "I can make him strong and well, but in my own way will I do it, and none must interfere."

Every day Queen Athenais marvelled at her son. From a little puling babe he became a strong and healthy child, but Isis spoke no word and none knew what she did. Athenais questioned her maidens, and they answered, "We know not what she

does, but this we know, that she feeds him not, and at night she
bars the doors of the hall of the pillar, and piles the fire high
with logs, and when we listen, naught can we hear but the twittering of a swallow."

Athenais was filled with curiosity and hid herself at night in
the great hall, and watched how Isis barred the doors and piled
the logs upon the fire till the flames rose high and scorching.
Then, sitting before the fire, she made a space between the
blazing logs, a space that glowed red and crimson, and in that
space she laid the child, and turning herself into the form of a
swallow, she circled round the pillar, mourning and lamenting,
and the lamentation was like the twittering of a swallow. Queen
Athenais shrieked and snatched the child from the fire, and
turned to flee. But before her stood Isis the Goddess, tall and
terrible.

"O foolish mother!" said Isis. "Why didst thou seize the child?
But a few days longer and all that is mortal in him would have
been burnt away, and as the Gods would he have been, immortal and for ever young."

A great awe fell upon the Queen, for she knew that she
looked upon one of the Gods. In humblest wise she and King
Malkander prayed the Goddess to accept a gift. All the riches of
Byblos were spread before her, but to her they were as naught.

"Give me," she said, "what this pillar holds and I shall be con-
tent." At once the workmen were summoned, and they took
down the pillar, and split it open, and lifted out the coffin. And
Isis took sweet spices and scented blossoms; these she strewed
upon the pillar, then wrapped it in fine linen and gave it to the
King and Queen. And all the people of Byblos worship it to this
day, because once it held the body of a god.

But Isis took the coffin on a boat and sailed away from Byblos,
and when the waves of the river Phaedrus, lashed by the wind,
threatened to sweep the coffin away, she dried up the water by
her magical spells. Then, in a solitary place, she opened the coffin, and, gazing upon the face of the dead God, she mourned
and lamented.

Now some say that when Isis left Byblos she took Diktys with
her, and that he fell out of the boat and was drowned. Others say

that the sound of her lamentation was so terrible in its grief that his heart broke and he died. But I think that he remained in Byblos; and because he had lain in the arms of the Divine Mother, and had passed through the purifying fire, he grew up to be a great and noble King, ruling his people wisely.

Then Isis hid the coffin and set out for the city of Pé, where it stood on the floating island and where her little son Harpocrates was safe under the care of Uazet, the Goddess of the North Country. And while she was away, Set came hunting wild boars with his dogs. He hunted by moonlight, for he loved the night, when all evil red things are abroad; and the air was filled with the whoop and halloa of the huntsman and the cries of the dogs as they rushed after their quarry. And as he dashed past, Set saw the painted chest, the colours glinting and gleaming in the moonlight.

At that sight, hatred and anger came upon him like a red cloud, and he raged like a panther of the South. He dragged the coffin from the place where it was hidden and forced it open; he seized the body and tore it into fourteen pieces, and by his mighty and divine strength he scattered the pieces throughout the land of Egypt. And he laughed and said, "It is not possible to destroy the body of a God, but I have done what is impossible, I have destroyed Osiris." And his laughter echoed across the world, and those who heard it fled trembling.

When Isis returned, she found naught but the broken coffin, and knew that Set had done this thing. All her search was now to begin again. She took a little shallop made of papyrus-reeds lashed together, and sailed through the marshes to look for the pieces of Osiris' body, and all the birds and beasts went with her to help her; and to this day the crocodiles will not touch a boat of papyrus-reeds, for they think it is the weary Goddess still pursuing her search.

A mighty and a cunning enemy was hers, and by wisdom only could he be overcome; therefore, wheresoever she found a fragment of the divine body, she built a beautiful shrine and performed the funeral rites as though she had buried it there. But in truth she took the fragments with her; and when, after long wanderings, she had found all, by the mighty power of her magic she united them again as one body. For when Horus the Child should be grown to manhood, then he should fight with Set and avenge his father; and after he had obtained the victory Osiris should live again.

But until that day Osiris lives in the Duat, where he rules the Dead wisely and nobly as he ruled the living when on earth. For though Horus fights with Set and the battles rage furiously, yet the decisive victory is not yet accomplished, and Osiris has never returned to earth again.

The Scorpions of Isis

I AM Isis, the great Goddess, the Mistress of Magic, the Speaker of Spells.

I came out of my house which my brother Set had given to me, for Thoth called to me to come, Thoth the twice great, mighty of truth in earth and in heaven. He called, and I came forth when Ra descended in glory to the western horizon of heaven, and it was evening.

And with me came the seven scorpions, and their names were Tefen and Befen, Mestet and Mestetef, Petet, Thetet, and Matet. Behind me were Tefen and Befen; on either side were Mestet and Mestetef; in front were Petet, Thetet, and Matet, clearing the way that none should oppose or hinder me. I called aloud to the scorpions, and my words rang through the air and entered into their ears, "Beware of the Black One, call not the Red One, look neither at children nor at any small helpless creature."

Then I wandered through the Land of Egypt, Tefen and Befen behind me, Mestet and Mestetef on either side of me, Petet, Thetet, and Matet before me; and we came to Per-sui, where the crocodile is God, and to the Town of the Two Sandals, which is the city of the Twin Goddesses. Here it is that the swamps and marshes of the North Country begin, where there are fields of papyrus-reeds, and where the marshmen dwell; from here to the Great Green Waters is the North Land.

Then we came near houses where the marsh-people dwelt, and the name of one of the women was "Glory," though some called her "Strength" also. She stood at her door, and from afar

27

she saw me coming, wayworn and weary, and I would fain have sat me down in her house to rest. But when I would have spoken to her, she shut the door in my face, for she feared the seven scorpions that were with me.

I went farther, and one of the marshwomen opened her door to me, and in her house I rested. But Mestet and Mestetef, Petet, Thetet, and Matet, and Befen also, they came together and laid their poison upon the sting of Tefen; thus the sting of Tefen had sevenfold power. Then returned Tefen to the house of the woman Glory, she who had closed her door against me; the door was still shut, but between it and the threshold was a narrow space. Through this narrow space crept Tefen and entered the house, and stung with a sting of sevenfold power the son of the woman Glory. So fierce and burning was the poison that the child died and fire broke out in the house.

Then the woman Glory cried and lamented, but no man hearkened to her, and Heaven itself sent water upon her house. A great marvel was this water from Heaven, for the time of the inundation was not yet.

Thus she mourned and lamented, and her heart was full of sorrow when she remembered how she had shut her door in my face when, weary and wayworn, I would have rested in her house. And the sound of her grief came to my ears, and my heart swelled with sorrow for her sorrow, and I turned back and went with her to where her dead child lay.

And I, Isis, the Mistress of Magic, whose voice can awake the dead, I called aloud the Words of Power, the Words that even the dead can hear. And I laid my arms upon the child that I might bring back Life to the lifeless. Cold and still he lay, for the sevenfold poison of Tefen was in him. Then did I speak magical spells to the poison of the scorpions, saying, "O poison of Tefen, come out of him and fall upon the ground! Poison of Befen, advance not, penetrate no farther, come out of him, and fall upon the ground! For I am Isis, the great Enchantress, the Speaker of Spells. Fall down, O poison of Mestet! Hasten not, poison of Mestetef! Rise not, poison of Petet and Thetet! Approach not, poison of Matet! For I am Isis, the great Enchantress, the Speaker of Spells. The child shall live, the poison shall die! As Horus is strong and well for me, his mother, so shall this child be strong and well for his mother!"

Then the child recovered, and the fire was quenched, and the rain from heaven ceased. And the woman Glory brought all her wealth, her bracelets and her neck-ornaments, her gold-work and silver-work, to the house of the marshwoman, and laid them at my feet in token of repentance that she had shut the door upon me when, weary and wayworn, I had come to her house.

And to this day men make dough of wheat-flour kneaded with salt and lay it upon the wound made by the sting of a scorpion, and over it they recite the Words of Power which I recited over the child of the woman Glory when the sevenfold poison was in him. For I am Isis, the great Enchantress, the Mistress of Magic, the Speaker of Spells.

The Black Pig

THE reason why the city of Pé was given to Horus, I know and
I will tell you.

Between Horus and Set there is enmity and hatred, war and
battle. Ever the fight goes on and the combatants rage furiously, and victory is not yet declared to either, though the Gods are
with Horus.

Now Set is cunning and crafty, and seeks to conquer by subtlety rather than by courage and skill in the fray; and such
power is his that he can take what form he will and deceive
both men and Gods. This is the power of Set, but the power of
Horus is not the same; for to Horus belong righteousness and
truth; deceit and falsehood are not in him. Whoso gazes into
the blue eyes of Horus can see the future reflected there, and
both Gods and men seek Horus to learn what shall come to
pass.

It came to the knowledge of Set that Ra would consult with
Horus, and it seemed to him that an opportunity was at hand to
injure Horus, so he took upon himself the form of a Black Pig.
Fierce was his aspect, long and sharp his tushes, and his colour
was the blackness of the thundercloud; savage and evil was his
look, and struck fear into the hearts of men.

Then came the Majesty of Ra to Horus and spoke to him saying, "Let me look in thine eyes and behold what is to come."
And he gazed into the eyes of Horus, and their colour was that
of the Great Green Waters when the summer sky shines upon
them. And while he gazed, the Black Pig passed by.

Ra knew not that it was the Evil God, and he cried out to

Horus and said, "Look at that Black Pig! Never have I seen one so huge and so fierce."

And Horus looked; neither did he know Set in this strange form, and thought it was a wild boar from the thickets of the North Country. Thus he was off his guard and unprotected against his enemy.

Then Set aimed a blow of fire at the eye of Horus, and Horus shouted aloud with the pain of the fire, and raged furiously, and cried, "It is Set, and he has smitten me with fire on the eyes."

But Set was no longer there, for he had conveyed himself away, and the Black Pig was seen no more. And Ra cursed the pig because of Set, and said, "Let the pig be an abomination to Horus." And to this day men sacrifice the pig when the Moon is at the full, because Set, the enemy of Horus, and the murderer of Osiris, took its form in order to injure the blue-eyed God. And for this reason also swineherds are unclean throughout the land of Egypt; never may they enter the temples and sacrifice to the Gods, and their sons and daughters may not marry with the worshippers of the Gods.

And when the eyes of Horus were healed, Ra gave to him the city of Pé, and he gave to him two divine brethren in the city of Pé, and two divine brethren in the city of Nekhen to be with him as everlasting judges. Then was the heart of Horus glad and he rejoiced, and at the joy of Horus the earth blossomed, and thunderclouds and rain were blotted out.

The Battles of Horus

IT was in the three hundred and sixty-third year of the reign of the God Ra-Horakhti upon earth that the great war happened between Horus and Set.

The Majesty of the God Ra, whom men call Ra-Horakhti also, was in Nubia with his army, a great and innumerable multitude of soldiers, footmen and horsemen, archers and chariots. He came in his Boat upon the river; the prow of the Boat was of palm-wood, its stern was of acacia-wood, and he landed at Thest-Hor, to the east of the Inner Waters. And to him came Horus of Edfu, he whose name is Harpooner and Hero, seeking for that Wicked One, Set, the murderer of Osiris. Long had he sought, but Set had ever eluded him.

The Majesty of Ra had gathered his forces, for Set had rebelled against him, and Horus was glad at the thought of battle, for he loved an hour of fighting more than a day of rejoicing. He entered into the presence of Thoth, the twice great, god of magic, and Thoth gave him the power to change himself into a great winged disk, a disk that glowed like a ball of fire, with great wings on either side like the colours of the sky at sunset when the blue shades from dark to light, and is shot with gold and flame. Men try to copy these hues when they carve the winged disk above the temple-doors, or make it into a breast-ornament of gold inlaid with turquoise and carnelian and lazuli.

Thus Horus, as a great winged disk, sat on the prow of the Boat of Ra, and his splendour flashed across the waters and fell upon his foes as they lay in ambush. Upon his glorious wings he rose into the air, and against his crafty enemies he made a curse, a curse terrible and fear-striking, saying, "Your eyes shall be blinded, and ye shall not see; and your ears shall be deaf, and ye shall not hear."

And at once, when each men looked at his neighbour, he saw a stranger; and when he heard his own familiar mother-tongue it sounded like a foreign language, and they cried out that they were betrayed, and that the enemy had come among them. They turned their weapons each against the other, and in the quickness of a moment many had ceased to live, and the rest had fled, while over them flew the gleaming Disk watching for Set. But Set was in the marshes of the North Country and these were but his advance-guard.

Then Horus flew back to Ra, and Ra embraced him and gave him a draught of wine mixed with water. And to this day men pour a libation of wine and water to Horus at this place in remembrance. When Horus had drunk the wine, he spoke to the Majesty of Ra and said, "Come and see thine enemies, how they lie overthrown in their blood." Ra came, and with him came Astarte, Mistress of Horses, driving her furious steeds; and they saw the corpse-strewn field where the army of Set had slain one another.

Now this is the first encounter in the South, but the last great battle was not yet.

Then the associates of Set came together and took counsel, and took upon themselves the likeness of crocodiles and hippopotamuses, for these great beasts can live under water and no human weapon can pierce their hides. They came up the river, the water swirling behind them, and rushed upon the Boat of Ra to overturn it. But Horus had gathered together his band of armourers and weapon-smiths, and they had prepared arrows and spears of metal, smelted and welded, hammered and shaped, with magical words and spells chanted over them. When the fierce beasts came up the river in waves of foam, the Followers of Horus drew their bowstrings and let fly their arrows, they cast their javelins, and charged with their spears. And the metal pierced the hides and reached the hearts, and of these wicked animals six hundred and fifty were slain, and the rest fled.

Now this is the second encounter in the South, but the last great battle was not yet.

The associates of Set fled, some up the river and some down the river; their hearts were weak and their feet failed for fear of Horus, the Harpooner, the Hero. And those whose faces were towards the South Land fled fastest, for Horus was at their back in the Boat of Ra; and with him came his Followers, their weapons in their hands.

At the south-east of Denderah, the city of Hathor, Horus saw the enemy, and he rushed upon them with his Followers, while Ra and Thoth watched the conflict as they waited in the Boat.

Then said the Majesty of Ra to Thoth, "See, how he wounds his enemies! See, how Horus of Edfu carries destruction among them!" And afterwards men built a shrine in this place in remembrance of the fight, and the Gods in the shrine were Ra and Min and Horus of Edfu.

Now this is the third encounter in the South, but the last great battle was not yet.

Then quickly they turned the Boat, and swiftly was it carried downstream, following the fugitives, whose faces were towards the North Land. For a night and a day they followed after, and at the north-east of Denderah Horus saw them. And he made haste, he and his Followers, and fell upon them, and slew them. Great and terrible was the slaughter as he drove them before him.

Thus was destroyed Set's army in the South in four great encounters, but the last great battle was not yet.

Now the allies of Set turned their faces towards the lake and towards the marshes of the sea. Horus came behind them in the Boat of Ra, and his form was the form of a great winged disk; and with him came his Followers, their weapons in their hands. Then Horus commanded silence, and silence was upon their mouths.

Four days and four nights were they upon the water seeking the enemy. But none did they find, for their foes had turned their shapes into the shapes of crocodiles and hippopotamuses, and lay hidden in the water. On the morning of the fifth day Horus saw them; at once he gave battle, and the air was filled with the noise of the combat, while Ra and Thoth watched the conflict as they waited in the Boat.

Then the Majesty of Ra cried aloud when he saw Horus like a devouring flame upon the battlefield, "See, how he casts his weapon against them, he kills them, he destroys them with his sword, he cuts them in pieces, he utterly defeats them! See and behold Horus of Edfu!" At the end of the fight Horus came back in triumph and he brought one hundred and forty-two prisoners to the Boat of Ra.

Now this is the first encounter in the North, but the last great battle was not yet.

For the enemies, who were upon the Northern Waters, turned their faces towards the canal to reach the sea, and they came to the Western Waters of Mert, where the Ally of Set had his dwelling. Behind them followed Horus, equipped with all his glittering weapons, and he went in the Boat of Ra, and Ra was in the Boat with eight of his train. They were upon the Northern Canal, and backwards and forwards they went, turning and re-turning, but nothing did they see or hear. Then they went northward for a night and a day and they came to the House of Berhu.

There Ra spoke to Horus and said, "Behold, thy enemies are gathered together at the Western Waters of Mert, where dwell the Allies of Set." And Horus of Edfu prayed the Majesty of Ra to come in his Boat against the Allies of Set.

Again they travelled to the northwards, where the never-setting Stars wheel round a certain point in the sky, and on the banks of the Western Waters of Mert were the Allies of Set, ready for battle. Then Horus of Edfu delayed not a moment, but rushed upon the foe, and with him came his Followers, their weapons in their hands. Death and destruction they dealt to right and to left till the enemy fled before them. When the conflict was over, they counted the prisoners; three hundred and eighty-one were taken, and these Horus slew before the Boat of Ra, and their weapons he gave to his Followers.

Now this is the second encounter in the North, but the last great battle was not yet.

And now, at last, Set himself came forth from his hiding-place. Fierce and savage he is, cunning and cruel; in his nature like a beast of prey, without ruth or pity; and men make his image with the head of a wild beast, for human feeling is to him unknown. From his hiding-place he came forth and he roared terribly. The earth and the heavens trembled at the sound of his roaring and at the words which he uttered, for he boasted that he would himself fight against Horus and destroy him as he had destroyed Osiris.

The wind bore the words of his boasting to Ra, and Ra said to Thoth the twice great, Lord of Magic and Wisdom, "Cause that these high words of the Terrible One be cast down."

Then Horus of Edfu sprang forward and rushed at his enemy, and a great fight raged. Horus cast his weapon and killed many, and his Followers fought also and prevailed. Out of the dust and the noise of the combat came Horus, dragging a prisoner; and the captive's arms were bound behind him, and the staff of Horus was tied across his mouth so that he could make no sound, and the weapon of Horus was at his throat.

Horus dragged him before the Majesty of Ra. And Ra spoke and said to Horus, "Do with him as thou wilt." Then Horus fell upon his enemy, and struck the weapon into his head and into his back, and cut off his head, and dragged the body about by the feet, and at last he cut the body into pieces. Thus did he treat the body of his adversary as Set had treated the body of Osiris. This took place on the seventh day of the first month of the season when the earth appears after the inundation. And the lake is called the Lake of Fighting to this day.

Now this is the third encounter in the North, but the last great battle was not yet.

For it was the Ally of Set whom Horus had slain, and Set himself was still alive, and he raged against Horus as a panther of the South. And he stood up and roared in the face of heaven, and his voice was the voice of thunder, and as he roared he changed himself into a great snake, and entered into the earth. None saw him go and none saw him change, but he was fighting against the Gods, and by their power and knowledge are they aware of what comes to pass, though no man tells them. And Ra said to Horus, "Set has transformed himself into a hissing snake and has entered the earth. We must cause that he never comes forth; never, never no more!"

The associates of Set took courage, knowing that their leader was alive, and they assembled again, and their boats filled the canal. The Boat of Ra went against them, and above the Boat shone the glory of the great winged Disk. When Horus saw the enemy gathered together in one place, he drove at them and routed them and slew them without number.

Now this is the fourth encounter in the North, but the last great battle was not yet.

Then Horus of Edfu remained in the Boat of Ra upon the canal for six days and six nights, watching for the enemy, but he saw none, for they lay as corpses in the water.

And to this day men make ceremonies in remembrance of the Battles of Horus on the first day of the first month of the inundation, on the seventh day of the first month of the appearing of the earth after the inundation, and on the twenty-first and twenty-fourth days of the second month of the earth's appearing. These days are kept holy at Ast-abt, which is at the south side of Anrudef, where is one of the graves of Osiris. And Isis made magical spells round Anrudef that no enemy might come near it; and the priestess of Anrudef is called "The Lady of Spells" to this day in remembrance; and the waters are called "The Waters of Seeking," for there it was that Horus sought for his foe.

And Horus sent out his Followers, and they hunted down the enemy, and brought in prisoners; one hundred and six from the East and one hundred and six from the West. These they slew before Ra in the sanctuaries.

Then Ra gave to Horus and his fighters two cities which are called the Mesen-cities to this day, for the Followers of Horus are Mesenti, the Metal-workers. In the shrines of the Mesen-cities Horus is the God, and his secret ceremonies are held on four days in the year. Great and holy are these days in the Mesen-cities, for they are in remembrance of the Battles of Horus which he fought against Set, the murderer of Osiris.

Now these enemies, they gathered again in the East, and they travelled towards Tharu. Then was launched the Boat of Ra to follow after them, and Horus of Edfu transformed himself into the likeness of a lion with the face of a man; his arms were like flint, and on his head was the Atef-crown, which is the white diadem of the South Land with feathers and horns, and on either side a crowned serpent. And he hastened after his enemies, and defeated them, and brought of prisoners one hundred and forty-two.

Then said Ra to Horus of Edfu, "Let us journey northwards to the Great Green Waters, and smite the foe there as we have smitten him in Egypt."

Northwards they went, and the enemy fled before them, and they reached the Great Green Waters, where the waves broke on the shore with the noise of thunder. Then Thoth arose and he stood in the midst of the Boat, and he chanted strange words over the boats and barges of Horus and his Followers, and the sea fell calm as the sound of the words floated across its waves. And there was silence on the Great Green Waters, for the wind was lulled, and naught was in sight save the boats of Ra and of Horus.

Then said the Majesty of Ra, "Let us sail round the whole extent of the land, let us sail to the South Land." And they knew that Ra was aware of the enemy. They made haste and sailed to the South Land by night, to the country of Ta-kens, and they came to the town of Shaïs, but until they reached Shaïs they saw naught of any enemy. Now Shaïs is on the border of Nubia, and in Nubia were the guards of the enemy.

Then Horus of Edfu changed himself into a great winged Disk with gleaming pinions outspread, and on either side of him came the goddesses Nekhbet and Uazet, and their form was the form of great hooded snakes with crowns upon their heads; on the head of Nekhbet was the white crown of the South Land, on the head of Uazet was the red crown of the North Land.

And the Gods in the Boat of Ra cried aloud and said, "See, O Thou who art twice great, he has placed himself between the two goddesses. Behold how he overthrows his adversaries and destroys them."

Now this is the encounter in Nubia, but the last great battle was not yet.

Then came Ra in his Boat and he moored at Thest-Hor, and

he gave commandment that in every temple throughout the Two Lands men should carve the Winged Disk, and on the right and left of the Disk should be Nekhbet and Uazet as great hooded snakes with crowns upon their heads. And the temple at the point of Thest-Hor is called "The House of Horus in the South" to this day in remembrance, and a great offering is made there to Ra and Horus. And Ra gave to Horus the province of the House of Fighting, and Ast-Abt, and the Mesen-cities of the East and the West, and Edfu of the North, and Tharu, and Gauti, and the Sea of Sailing, and Upper Shasu, and Edfu-of-the-House-of-Ra. And from the lake south of Edfu-of-the-House-of-Ra they bring water to the two Houses of the King on the day of the Sed-festival. And Isis carried Ar-stone of sand to Thest-Hor—Ar-stone of the Star was it; and in every place in the South Land to which Horus went, there is Ar-stone found to this day.

Now some say that the last great battle is still to come, and that in the end Horus will kill Set, and that Osiris and all the Gods will reign on earth when their enemy is utterly destroyed. But others say that the battle is already ended and that Horus slew the great and wicked Foe who had wrought misery and calamity to all.

And this is what they say: After months and years Horus the Child grew to manhood. Then came Set with his allies, and he challenged Horus in the presence of Ra. And Horus came forth, his Followers with him in their boats, with their armour, and their glittering weapons with handles of worked wood, and their cords, and their spears.

And Isis made golden ornaments for the prow of the boat of Horus, and she laid them in their places with magic words and spells, saying, "Gold is at the prow of thy boat, O Lord of Mesen, Horus, Chieftain of the boat, the great boat of Horus, the boat of rejoicing. May the valour of Ra, the strength of Shu, power and fear be around thee. Thou art victorious, O son of Osiris, son of Isis, for thou fightest for the throne of thy father."

Then Set took upon himself the form of a red hippopotamus, great and mighty, and he came from the South Land with his Allies, travelling to the North Land to meet Horus of Edfu. And at Elephantine, Set stood up and spoke a great curse against Horus of Edfu and against Isis, and said, "Let there come a great wind, even a furious north-wind and a raging tempest"; and the sound of his voice was like thunder in the East of the sky. His words were cried from the southern heaven and rolled back to the northern heaven, a word and a cry from Set, the enemy of Osiris and the Gods.

At once a storm broke over the boats of Horus and his Followers, the wind roared, and the water was lashed into great waves, and the boats were tossed like straws. But Horus held on his way; and through the darkness of the storm and the foam of the waves gleamed the golden prow like the rays of the sun.

And Horus took upon himself the form of a young man; his height was eight cubits; in his hand he held a harpoon, the blade was four cubits, the shaft twenty cubits, and a chain of sixty cubits was welded to it. Over his head he brandished the weapon as though it were a reed, and he launched it at the great red hippopotamus which stood in the deep waters, ready to destroy Horus and his Followers when the storm should wreck their boats.

And at the first cast the weapon struck deep into the head of the great red hippopotamus and entered the brain. Thus died Set, that great and wicked One, the enemy of Osiris and the Gods.

And to this day the priests of Horus of Edfu, and the King's daughters, and the women of Busiris and the women of Pé chant a hymn and strike the drum for Horus in triumph.

And this is their song: "Rejoice, O women of Busiris! Rejoice, O women of Pé! Horus has overthrown his enemies!

"Exult, dwellers in Edfu! Horus, the great God, Lord of heaven, has smitten the enemy of his father!

"Eat ye the flesh of the vanquished, drink ye his blood, burn ye his bones in the flame of the fire. Let him be cut in pieces, and let his bones be given to the cats, the fragments of him to the reptiles.

"O Horus, the Striker, the great One of Valour, the Slayer, the Chief of the Gods, the Harpooner, the Hero, the only begotten, Captor of captives, Horus of Edfu, Horus the Avenger!

"He has destroyed the wicked One, he has made a whirlpool with the blood of his enemy, his shaft has made a prey. Behold ye, see ye Horus at the prow of his boat. Like Ra, he shines on the horizon. He is decked in green linen, in binding linen, in fine linen and byssus. The double diadem is upon thy head, the two serpents upon thy brow, O Horus the Avenger!

"Thy harpoon is of metal, the shaft is of the sycamore of the desert, the net is woven by Hathor of the Roses. Thou hast aimed to the right, thou hast cast to the left. We give praise to thee to the height of heaven, for thou hast chained the wickedness of thine enemy. We give praise to thee, we worship thy majesty, O Horus of Edfu, Horus the Avenger!"

The Beer of Heliopolis

Now the Majesty of Ra reigned over the Two Lands. He was the second king of Egypt, and in his reign peace was on earth, and harvests were so plentiful that to this day men speak of the good things which "happened in the time of Ra." By his own power he created himself, and he created heaven and earth, gods and men, and he ruled over them all.

For hundreds and hundreds of years he ruled until he waxed old, and men no longer feared him, but laughed and said, "Look at Ra! He is old, his bones are like silver, his flesh like gold, and his hair like true lapis lazuli."

Then Ra was wroth when he heard their jests and their laughter, and he called to those who were in his train, "Summon hither my daughter, the apple of my eye, and summon also the gods Shu and Tefnut, Geb and Nut, and the great god Nun, whose dwelling is in the waters of the sky. Do my bidding secretly lest men should hear you and see you, for then would they be afraid and hide themselves."

In secret went the messengers, very softly they came to summon the gods and goddesses. Secretly and softly came the gods and goddesses to the Mansion of Ra in the Hidden Place. Naught did men see or hear; and they laughed again at Ra, not knowing the punishment that should fall upon them.

On each side of the throne came the gods and goddesses, and they bowed before the Majesty of Ra with their foreheads to the ground, saying, "Speak that we may hear."

Then said Ra to Nun, the great god whose dwelling is in the waters of the sky, "O eldest of the gods and all ye ancestor-gods!

Behold the men whom I have created, how they speak against me. Tell me what ye would that I should do to them, for verily I will not slay them till I have heard your words."

And Nun, the great god whose dwelling is in the waters of the sky, made answer, "My son Ra, greatest of gods, mightiest of kings, thy throne is set fast, and thy fear will be upon all the world when thou sendest out thy daughter, the apple of thine eye, against those who attack thee."

The Majesty of Ra spoke again, "Lo, they will flee to the deserts and the mountains and hide themselves, if fear falls upon their hearts on account of their jests and laughter; and in the deserts and mountains none can find them."

Then said the gods and goddesses, bowing before him with their foreheads on the ground, "Send forth thy daughter, the apple of thine eye, against them."

And at once there came the daughter of Ra. Sekhmet is she called, and Hathor, fiercest of the goddesses; like a lion she rushes on her prey, slaughter is her delight, and her pleasure is in blood.

At her father's bidding she entered the Two Lands to slay those who had rebelled against the Majesty of Ra, and had turned their rebellion to jest and laughter. In the land of Tamery she killed them, and on the mountains which lie to the east and west of the great river. To and fro she hastened, slaying all who crossed her path, and before her fled the rebels against Ra.

And Ra looked forth upon the earth and cried to his daughter, the apple of his eye, "Come in peace, O Hathor! Hast thou done that which I gave thee to do?"

And Hathor laughed as she answered, and her laugh was the terrible voice of the lioness as she tears her prey. "By thy life, O Ra," she cried, "I work my will upon men, and my heart rejoices."

For many nights the river ran red, and the goddess waded in the blood of men, and her feet were red as she strode through the land of Egypt as far as Henen-seten.

Then Ra looked forth upon the earth again, and his heart was filled with pity for men, though they had rebelled against him. But none could stop the ruthless goddess, not even the Majesty of Ra himself; of herself must she cease to slay, for neither gods nor men could compel her. By subtlety alone could this be accomplished.

Ra gave command, saying, "Call hither to me messengers who are swift as the blast of the storm wind." And when they were brought, he said, "Run to Elephantine, hasten, go quickly, and bring back to me the fruit that causes sleep. Be swift, be swift, for all this must be accomplished ere the day dawn."

The messengers hastened, and their speed was the speed of a blast of the storm-wind. They came to Elephantine, where the great river rages among the rocks that bar its passage; they took the fruit that causes sleep, and with the fleetness of the wind they brought it to Ra. Crimson and scarlet was the fruit, and its juice was the colour of man's blood; and the messengers carried to it Heliopolis, the city of Ra.

Then the women of Heliopolis crushed barley and made beer, and with the beer they mixed the juice of the fruit that causes sleep, and the beer became the colour of blood. Seven thousand measures of beer did they make, and in haste they brewed it, for the night was drawing to a close and the day was about to break. In haste came the Majesty of Ra, and all the gods and goddesses, who were with him, to Heliopolis to inspect the beer. Ra saw that it was like human blood, and he said, "Very good is this beer. By this I can protect mankind."

At the dawning of the day, he gave command, "Carry this beer to the place where men and women have been slain, and pour it out upon the fields before the beauty of the night has passed." So they poured it out upon the fields. Four palms deep it lay upon the ground, and its colour was the colour of blood.

In the morning came the fierce Sekhmet, ready to slay, and as she passed by she looked to this side and that, watching for her prey. But no living thing did she see, only the fields that lay four palms deep in the beer that was the colour of blood. Then she laughed with the laugh like the roar of a lioness, for she thought it was the blood she had shed. And she stooped and drank. Again and again she drank, and she laughed the more, for the juice of the fruit that causes sleep mounted to her brain, and no longer could she see to slay by reason of the juice of that fruit.

Then the Majesty of Ra said to her, "Come in peace, O sweet one." And to this day the maidens of Amu are called "Sweet Ones" in remembrance.

And the Majesty of Ra spoke again to the goddess, saying, "For thee shall be prepared drinks from the fruits that cause sleep; every year shall these be made at the great Festival of the New Year, and the number of them shall be according to the number of the priestesses who serve me."

And to this day, on the festival of Hathor, drinks are made of the fruits that cause sleep, according to the number of the priestesses of Ra, in remembrance of the protection of mankind from the fury of the goddess.

The Name of Ra

Now the Majesty of Ra was the creator of heaven and earth, of gods, men, and cattle, of fire, and the breath of life; and he ruled over gods and men. And Isis saw his might, the might that reached over heaven and earth, before which all gods and men bowed; and she longed in her heart for that power, that thereby she should be greater than the gods and have dominion over men.

There was but one way to obtain that power. By the knowledge of his own name did Ra rule, and none but himself knew that secret name. Whosoever could learn the secret, to that one—god or man—would belong the dominion over all the world, and even Ra himself must be in subjection. Jealously did Ra guard his secret, and kept it ever in his breast, lest it should be taken from him, and his power diminished.

Every morning Ra came forth in his glory at the head of his train from the horizon of the East, journeying across the sky, and in the evening they came to the horizon of the West, and the Majesty of Ra sank in his glory to lighten the thick darkness of the Duat. Many, many times had Ra made the journey, so many times that now he had waxed old. Very aged was Ra, and the saliva ran down from his mouth and fell upon the earth.

Then Isis took earth and mixed it with the saliva, and she kneaded the clay and moulded it, and formed it into the shape of a snake, the shape of the great hooded snake that is the emblem of all goddesses, the royal serpent which is upon the brow of the Kings of Egypt. No charms or magic spells did she use, for in the snake was the divine substance of Ra himself. She

46

took the snake and laid it hidden in the path of Ra, the path on which he travelled in journeying from the eastern to the western horizon of heaven.

In the morning came Ra and his train in their glory journeying to the western horizon of heaven, where they enter the Duat and lighten the thick darkness. And the serpent shot out its pointed head which was shaped like a dart, and its fangs sank into the flesh of Ra, and the fire of its poison entered into the God, for the divine substance was in the serpent.

Ra cried aloud, and his cry rang through the heavens from the eastern to the western horizon; across the earth it rang, and gods and men alike heard the cry of Ra. And the gods who follow in his train said to him, "What aileth thee? What aileth thee?"

But Ra answered never a word, he trembled in all his limbs, and his teeth chattered, and naught did he say, for the poison spread over his body as Hapi spreads over the land, when the waters rise above their banks at the time of the overflowing of the river.

When he had become calm, he called to those who followed him and said, "Come to me, ye whom I created. I am hurt by a grievous thing. I feel it, though I see it not, neither is it the creation of my hands, and I know not who has made it. Never, never have I felt pain like this, never, never has there been an injury worse than this. Who can hurt me? For none know my secret name, that name which was spoken by my father and by my mother, and hidden in me that none might work withcraft upon me. I came forth to look upon the world which I had made, I passed across the Two Lands when something—I know not what—struck me. Is it fire? Is it water? I burn, I shiver, I tremble in all my limbs. Call to me the children of the gods, they who have skill in healing, they who have knowledge of magic, they whose power reaches to heaven."

Then came all the gods with weeping and mourning and lamentations; their power was of no avail against the serpent, for in it the divine substance was incorporated. With them came Isis the Healer, the Mistress of Magic, in whose mouth is the Breath of Life, whose words destroy disease and awake the dead.

She spoke to the Majesty of Ra and said. "What is this, O

divine Father? what is this? Has a snake brought pain to thee? Has the creation of thy hand lifted up its head against thee? Lo, it shall be overthrown by the might of my magic, I will drive it out by means of thy glory."

Then the Majesty of Ra answered, "I passed along the appointed path, I crossed over the Two Lands, when a serpent that I saw not struck me with its fangs. Was it fire? Was it water? I am colder than water, I am hotter than fire, I tremble in all my limbs, and the sweat runs down my face as down the faces of men in the fierce heat of summer."

And Isis spoke again, and her voice was low and soothing, "Tell me thy Name, O divine Father, thy true Name, thy secret Name, for he only can live who is called by his name."

Then the Majesty of Ra answered, "I am the Maker of heaven and earth, I am the Establisher of the mountains, I am the Creator of the waters, I am the Maker of the secrets of the two Horizons, I am Light and I am Darkness, I am the Maker of Hours, the Creator of Days, I am the Opener of Festivals, I am the Maker of running streams, I am the Creator of living flame. I am Khepera in the morning, Ra at noontide, and Atmu in the evening."

But Isis held her peace; never a word did she speak, for she knew that Ra had told her the names that all men know; his true Name, his secret Name, was still hidden in his breast. And the power of the poison increased, and ran through his veins like burning flame.

After a silence she spoke again. "Thy Name, thy true Name, thy secret Name, was not among those. Tell me thy Name that the poison may be driven out, for only he whose name I know can be healed by the might of my magic." And the power of the poison increased, and the pain was as the pain of living fire.

Then the Majesty of Ra cried out and said, "Let Isis come with me, and let my Name pass from my breast to her breast."

And he hid himself from the gods that followed in his train. Empty was the Boat of the Sun, empty was the great throne of the God, for Ra had hidden himself from his Followers and from the creations of his hands.

When the Name came forth from the heart of Ra to pass to

the heart of Isis, the goddess spoke to Ra and said, "Bind thyself with an oath, O Ra, that thou wilt give thy two eyes unto Horus." Now the two Eyes of Ra are the sun and the moon, and men call them the Eyes of Horus to this day.

Thus was the Name of Ra taken from him and given to Isis, and she, the great Enchantress, cried aloud the Word of Power, and the poison obeyed, and Ra was healed by the might of his Name.

And Isis, the great One, Mistress of the Gods, Mistress of Magic, she is the skilful Healer, in her mouth is the Breath of Life, by her words she destroys pain, and by her power she awakes the dead.

The Regions of Night
and Thick Darkness

WHEN the world came into being, there were two rivers, the river of Egypt and the river of the sky. Great is the Nile, the river of Egypt, rising in his two caverns in the South beyond the cataract, flooding the land of Egypt and bringing joy and good harvests to Ta-mery. Great and mighty is the river of the sky, flowing across the heavens and through the Duat, the world of night and of thick darkness, and on that river floats the Boat of Ra. Boat of Millions of Years is its name, but men call it the Manzet Boat in the dawn, when Ra rises in splendour on the eastern horizon of heaven; the Mesektet Boat is it called in the evening, when Ra enters in glory within the portals of the Duat, where the mountain of Manu lifts its peaks to the western sky. On the western horizon is the mountain of Manu, and on the eastern horizon the mountain of Bakhu; vast and huge are they, raising their crests above the earth, and the sky rests upon their summits. And on the topmost peak of the mountain of Bakhu dwells a serpent; thirty cubits in length is he, and his scales are of flint and of glittering metal. He guards the mountain and the Great Green Waters, and none can pass by him save Ra in his Boat.

In the evening Ra descends in majesty to the Western horizon of heaven, to the portals of the Duat at the Gap of Abydos. Splendid is the Mesektet Boat, glorious its trappings, and its colours are of amethyst and emerald, jasper and turquoise, lazuli and the lustre of gold. At the Gap of Abydos waits a company of gods to prepare the Boat for the journey through the

Duat, the land of night and of thick darkness. Stripped is the Boat of its splendour, bare and without glory is it when it passes through the portals of the Duat, and in it is the body of Ra, lifeless and dead.

Then the gods take the great towing-ropes; slowly the Boat moves along the river. The portals of the Duat are flung wide, and the twelve goddesses of the night take their place upon the Boat to guide it through the gloom and perils of the Duat; pilots of the river are they, and without them not Ra himself could pass through unscathed.

"Watercourse of Ra" is the name of the first country of the Duat. Sombre is this land, yet not wholly dark; for on either side the river are six serpents, coiled and with heads erect, and the breath of their mouths is a flame of fire. In the cabin of the Boat is Ra, dead and lifeless; in the prow are Up-uaut, the Opener of the Ways, and Sa, and the goddess of the hour. Round about the cabin are a company of gods; these are they who guard Ra from all perils and dangers, and from the attack of the abominable Apep.

Slowly goes the Boat of Ra, passing through the Duat, to regions of thick darkness, of horror and dismay, where the dead have their habitations, and Apep lies in wait for the coming of Ra. Thus passes the first hour of the night, and the second hour is at hand.

At the entrance of every country of the Duat is a gate; tall are the walls, and narrow is the passage; upon the walls are spearheads, sharp and pointed, that no man may climb over. The door of the gate is of wood, turning on a pivot, and a monstrous snake guards the door. None may pass by him save those only to whom his name is known. At the turn of the passage are two great hooded snakes, the one above, the other below. The breath of their mouths is fire and poison mingled; through the narrow portal on every side they send forth streams of flame and venom. At either end of the passage stands a warder, keeping watch.

Then the goddess of the first hour makes way for the goddess of the second hour, and she calls aloud the name of the Guardian of the gate. Flung wide are the portals, the fire and poison cease, and the Boat of Ra passes through.

"Ur-nes" do we name this second country of the Duat, but the Hanebu and those who inhabit the isles of the Great Green Waters call it Ouranos. The river is wide and bears on its dark waters four shallops; no oars have they, neither masts nor rudders, but float upon the stream and are carried by the current. Mysterious and strange are they, and the shadowy shapes which fill them have forms like the forms of men. In this country Ra is Lord and King, and those who live here are in peace, for none can pass the great hooded snakes who guard the gates, whose breath is mingled flame and venom. Happy are those who inhabit this land, for here dwell the spirits of the corn, Besa and Nepra and Tepu-yn. These are they who make the wheat and barley to flourish and cause the fruits of the earth to increase.

Slowly goes the Boat of Ra, passing through the Duat, through regions of thick darkness, of horror and dismay, where the dead have their habitation, and Apep lies in wait for the coming of Ra. Thus passes the second hour of the night, and the third hour is at hand. Then the goddess of the second hour makes way for the goddess of the third hour, and she calls aloud the name of the Guardian of the gate. Flung wide are the portals, and the Boat of Ra passes through.

"Watercourse of the only God" is the name of the third country of the Duat, and here in the beautiful Amentet is the Kingdom of Osiris. On either side of the river are the great shapes of the gods surrounding the form of Osiris himself. Enthroned is he, appearing in splendour as king, with the White Crown of the South Land and the Red Crown of the North Land upon his head.

Great is Osiris, god of the dead, for all who die come before him for judgment, and their hearts are weighed in the balance against the feather of Truth. His throne is set upon a running stream, clear and deep, and from the waters rises a single lotus-blossom, the colour of the sky at morning. Upon the blossom stand the four Children of Horus, they who assist Osiris at the Judgment, who protect the bodies of the dead. To them belong the South and the North, the West and the East, and the four great goddesses are their protectors. They stand upon the lotus-blossom and their faces are towards Osiris; the first has the face of a man, the second the face of an ape, the third the face of a jackal, and the fourth the face of a bird of prey. This is the hour which evil-doers fear; by their own actions are they judged, and naught can avail them. Heavy is the heart of the evil-doer and drags down the scale; lower and lower it sinks till it reaches the jaws of Amemt, the Devourer of Hearts. Then is the evil-doer driven forth into the thick darkness of the Duat, to dwell with the abominable Apep and to fall at last into the Pits of Fire.

But some there are who have wrought righteousness upon earth; who have hurt no man by fraud or violence; who have succoured the widow, the orphan, and the shipwrecked mariner; who have given food to the hungry and clothes to the naked; who have not stirred up strife, nor caused the shedding of tears. When these come to the Judgment of Osiris, and their hearts are put in the balance, then is the feather of Truth the heavier. The scale with the feather sinks down, and the scale with the heart rises up. Then does Thoth, the twice-great, take the heart and place it again in the breast of the man, and Horus takes him by the hand and leads him to the foot of the throne of Osiris that he may dwell in the kingdom of Osiris for ever and for ever-more. And now only can he see the most pure and truly holy Osiris, for "the souls of men are not able to participate of the divine nature whilst they are encompassed about with bodies and passions. . . . When they are freed from these impediments and remove into those purer and unseen regions . . . 'tis then that this God becomes their Leader and King; upon him they wholly depend, still beholding without satiety, and still ardently longing after that beauty, which 'tis not possible for man to express or think."*

Slowly goes the Boat of Ra, passing through the Duat, to regions of thick darkness, of horror and dismay, where the abominable Apep lies in wait for the coming of Ra, and where the Pits of Fire are prepared for the wicked. Thus passes the third hour of the night, and the fourth hour is at hand. Then the goddess of the third hour makes way for the goddess of the fourth hour, and she calls aloud the name of the Guardian of the

*Plutarch, *De Iside et Osiride* (Squire's translation).

gate. Flung wide are the portals, and the Boat of Ra passes through.

"Living one of forms" is the name of the fourth country of the Duat, and Sokar has dominion in this land. Dreary is the waste of sand, limitless the desert, gloomy and sombre the landscape. No blade of grass is seen, no tree, no herbage; naught grows, naught lives, save monstrous many-headed serpents, gliding along the ground or creeping upon legs. Terrible are they of aspect as they writhe and turn and hiss and roar; they raise their hideous crests on high and hold their dusky wings outspread. But their anger is not towards Ra, and he passes safely through their midst.

Engulfed is the great river and lost beneath the shifting sands, and where it ran is now a deep ravine. The walls of rock rise high and steep, and ever the way winds and turns between the rocks. Men call this place Re-stau, the Mouth of the Tomb. Even in this gloomy desert Osiris has dominion; Lord of Re-stau is he called, therefore none need fear when traversing the narrow path. And now the Boat of Ra can no longer float upon the water, but is changed into a great and mighty serpent with glittering scales. At the prow is a serpent's head with eyes watchful and fierce, at the stern is a serpent's head with poison-fangs prepared. Over the sand it glides as a boat glides over the water.

Slowly goes the Boat of Ra, passing through the Duat, through regions of thick darkness, of horror and dismay, to the place where Apep lies in wait for the coming of Ra. Thus passes the fourth hour of the night, and the fifth hour is at hand. Then the goddess of the fourth hour makes way for the goddess of the fifth hour, and she calls aloud the name of the Guardian of the gate. Flung wide are the portals, and the Boat of Ra passes through.

"Hidden" is the name of the fifth country of the Duat, and in this dark and gloomy region dwells Sokar, its Lord and King, god of those who are buried. Beside a turn of the winding way is his dwelling deep below the ground; above it rises a high mountain of sand. Guarding it on either side are two sphinxes; lions are they in their bodies, with the faces of men; and their claws are outstretched like the talons of a beast of prey. In the midst lies

a serpent with three heads, and between his wings stands Sokar
in the form of a man with the head of a hawk. Savage and fierce
as a hawk is Sokar, and terrible is the punishment he metes out
to those who rebel against him. Hard by his dwelling is a lake
where the water boils and bubbles with heat as water boils in a
pot. Into the boiling lake are cast the rebels, and they cry to Ra
for help, but Ra lies cold and lifeless, waiting for the coming of
Khepera, and their cries are unheeded while the Boat passes on
its way.

On the farther wall of the ravine is a high and vaulted building, the home of Night and Darkness. Two birds cling on either
side, and round about it glides a two-headed serpent. He lifts his
savage heads, and his poison is ever ready to strike the rash
intruder who should dare to try to pass. Faithful is his watch, for
in the home of Night and Darkness lives Khepera, the great
Soul of the universe, he whose emblem is the beetle, the god of
resurrection. In the form of a scarab he watches the coming of
Ra, and he flies upon the Boat and awaits there the time when
he shall bring Life back to the god. And now through the thick
darkness along the narrow passage falls a gleam of light; the
Morning Star stands by the gate to lead the Boat onwards; for in
the darkest of the night is a promise of the coming day.

Slowly goes the Boat of Ra, passing through the Duat,
through regions of thick darkness, of terror and dismay, to the
place where the abominable Apep lies in wait for the coming of
Ra. Thus passes the fifth hour of the night, and the sixth hour is
at hand. Then the goddess of the fifth hour makes way for the
goddess of the sixth hour, and she calls aloud the name of the
Guardian of the gate. Flung wide are the portals, and the Boat
of Ra passes through.

"Abyss of waters" is the name of the sixth country of the Duat,
and Osiris has dominion over it, Osiris, the great god, Lord of
the city of Daddu, the living King, Creator of men, of cattle, and
of the green things which grow upon the earth, Osiris, to whom
all men bow in praise and adoration.

The river rises out of the sand again, and the Boat floats upon
its waters, and those who are in it rejoice, for the hours of the
night are passing away. On the banks of the river are the great

shapes of the gods, mysterious and wonderful; nine sceptres of sovereignty stand there also, and a monstrous lion looms through the darkness, faintly seen in the light which comes from the Boat of Ra. Three shrines stand beside the river, and a serpent whose breath is flame guards each one. Mystic and strange are the forms within the shrines, and to man it is not given to know the meaning of them; in one is a human head, in another the wing of a bird, in the third the hind part of a lion. Here also lives the great coiled serpent with five heads, and within his coils lies Khepera, god of resurrection. On his head he places the scarab, beneath his feet is the sign of flesh; thus does he send Life into the dead, and thus will he re-vivify Ra. For this is the farthest point of the Duat, and beyond the gate lies the way to the sunrise.

Slowly goes the Boat of Ra, passing through the Duat, through regions of thick darkness, of horror and dismay, where the abominable Apep lies in wait for the coming of Ra. Thus passes the sixth hour of the night, and the seventh hour is at hand. Then the goddess of the sixth hour makes way for the goddess of the seventh hour, and she calls aloud the name of the Guardian of the gate. Flung wide are the portals, and the Boat of Ra passes through.

"Secret cavern" is the name of the seventh country of the Duat. Full of danger and peril is it, for the abominable Apep dwells in this land. As a great and monstrous serpent does he appear and with wide-open mouth he swallows the waters of the river, that the Boat may be wrecked and that Ra may perish. Then would the earth belong to the powers of darkness, and evil and wickedness would overcome the gods.

But in the prow of the Boat stands Isis, the great enchantress, whose magic none can withstand; Isis, the greatest of the goddesses, she who can raise the dead, and to whom all mankind pay love and reverence. With arms outstretched, she recites the Words of Power; calling aloud across the dark river. Over the body of Ra, the serpent Mehen casts his protecting coils, for now is the time of danger.

On a sandbank in the midst of the river lies the abominable Apep. Four hundred and fifty cubits long is the sandbank; the coils of Apep cover it so that naught can be seen but the river around him. Loud does he hiss and roar, and the Duat is filled with the thunder of his voice, yet Isis flinches not, nor does she cease her incantations and the magical movements of her hands. Her spells prevail and the abominable Apep lies helpless on the sand. Then Selk and Her-desuf leap from the Boat of Ra and bind him with cords, and with sharp knives they pierce his flesh, hoping to destroy him. But Apep is immortal, and every night will he await and attack the Boat of Ra. Yet Selk and Her-desuf hold him fast while the Boat continues on its way, past the great sandbanks, where he writhes and twists and struggles to get free, but the cords are strong and the knives are sharp and his efforts are in vain.

Onward goes the Boat to the burial-places of the gods. These stand beside the river; high mounds of sand are they, over each mound is a building, and at each end the head of a man watches the passing of Ra.

Softly goes the Boat of Ra, passing through the Duat, moving through the darkness to the sunrise and the day. Thus passes the seventh hour of the night, and the eighth hour is at hand. Then the goddess of the seventh hour makes way for the goddess of the eighth hour, and she calls aloud the name of the Guardian of the gate. Flung wide are the portals, and the Boat of Ra passes through.

"Sarcophagus of the gods" is the name of the eighth country of the Duat, for here dwell the dead gods. Dead and buried are they, embalmed and bandaged as men embalm and bandage the dead upon earth. They cry aloud salutations to Ra as he passes, calling to him across the vast expanse, but so far away are they that the sound of their voices is as the roaring of savage bulls, as the cry of birds of prey, as the wail of mourners, as the murmur of bees. Before the Boat go nine Followers of the Gods; strange are their forms, mysterious and wonderful, like naught that is upon the earth. In front of them march the four souls of Tatanen in the likeness of rams, great and fierce, with horns widespreading and sharp-pointed. The first is crowned with high upstanding plumes, the second with the Red crown of the North Land, the third with the White crown of the South Land, the fourth with the glittering disk of the sun. Ancient is Tatanen, dweller in Memphis, where the abode of Ptah is on the south of the wall.

Softly goes the Boat of Ra, passing through the Duat, moving through the darkness to the sunrise and the day. Thus passes the eighth hour of the night, and the ninth hour is at hand. Then the goddess of the eighth hour makes way for the goddess of the ninth hour, and she calls aloud the name of the Guardian of the gate. Flung wide are the portals, and the Boat of Ra passes through.

"Procession of images" is the name of the ninth country of the Duat. Full and strong runs the river, and the Boat is borne forward upon the rushing stream. Twelve star-gods guard the Boat, with paddles in their hands, ready to help the Boat in case of need. Thick darkness broods not upon this land, for twelve great hooded snakes lie coiled upon the bank, and the breath of their mouths is a flame of fire, gleaming upon the dark water and upon those who dwell in the Duat. Three shallops float upon the sombre river; strange is the shape of these shallops, not like the boats of men; and the shadowy forms within them are in the likeness of a cow, of a ram, and of the soul of a man. From them the dwellers in this land receive the offerings which are made to them upon the earth. Then the star-gods break into singing; and the twelve goddesses and the weaving gods and the dwellers in this land chant the glory and honour of Ra, praising the Lord of the Boat, the Maker of earth and of heaven. With joy and singing they follow the appointed path.

Onward goes the Boat of Ra, passing through the Duat, travelling to the sunrise and the light of open day. Thus passes the ninth hour of the night, and the tenth hour is at hand. Then the goddess of the ninth hour makes way for the goddess of the tenth hour, and she calls aloud the name of the Guardian of the gate. Flung wide are the portals, and the Boat of Ra passes through.

"Abyss of waters, lofty of banks" is the name of the tenth country of the Duat, and the ruler is Ra. The dwellers in this land come to meet their king as he passes by upon the swelling river. Deep and full and strong runs the stream, and the Boat is

borne forward upon the rushing current. Divine warriors armed
with glittering weapons of war are a guard for their king; light is
on their faces like the light of the sun. By the side of the river
are four goddesses; upon the darkness they cast beams of light,
making bright the way of Ra upon the gloomy river. Before the
Boat of Ra moves the Star of Morning in the form of a double-
headed serpent walking upon legs, and upon his heads are the
crowns of the South Land and the North Land; between his
coils is the great hawk of the sky; Leader of Heaven is his name,
for the stars of heaven follow him, but men call him Hesper and
Lucifer also. In a shallop on the stream is a snake, Life of the
Earth is he called, and he watches in the Duat against the enemies of Ra.

The greatest of all the countries of the Duat is this, for in this
realm of wonder and mystery Khepera joins himself to Ra, and
Ra himself is created anew. Yet the dead body of Ra remains in
the Boat; but his soul is united to the soul of Khepera.

Onward goes the Boat of Ra, passing through the Duat, travelling to the sunrise and the light of open day. Thus passes the
tenth hour of the night and the eleventh hour is at hand. Then
the goddess of the tenth hour makes way for the goddess of the
eleventh hour, and she calls aloud the name of the Guardian of
the gate. Flung wide are the portals, and the Boat of Ra passes
through.

"Mouth of the cavern" is the name of the eleventh country of
the Duat, and Ra is its ruler. Low has the river fallen and slug-
gishly it runs, and the Boat is drawn onwards by the gods; not
with cords do they tow it, but with the body of the great serpent
Mehen, the protector of Ra. On the prow of the Boat is a fiery
star, but its light is not redder than the strange and lurid glow
which fills this land; terrible and red is it and the sight of it is full
of horror. This is the region feared by evil-doers, for their punishment awaits them here. Far and near are pits of fire; goddesses, whose breath is flame, guard the pits, holding in their
hands gleaming swords of fire. With their knives do they torment the wicked and cast them into the pits of flame till they
perish utterly. Horus stands by and beholds their torments, for
these are the enemies of Osiris and of Ra, doers of evil upon the

earth and blasphemers of the gods. No help can come to them, no escape is possible; doomed are they by their own actions to the sword and fire. And the smoke and flame of their torment rise up in the Duat.

On the far side of the river are the stars; Shedu is there in the fashion of a snake; scarlet and crimson is he, and the stars which form his body are ten in number. There also a shape is seen, mysterious and wonderful; like a winged snake with legs does he appear, and between the wings is the shadowy likeness of a man. Men call him Atmu, dweller in Heliopolis; ancient is Atmu, more ancient than Ra himself; and he sends the sweet breezes of the North Wind upon the land of Egypt. On either side of him the Eyes of Horus show dimly in the faint and lurid light. And now springs up the breeze of morning; gentle is it and slight, but with it comes the promise of the day.

Onward goes the Boat of Ra, passing through the Duat, travelling to the sunrise and the light of open day. Thus passes the eleventh hour, and the twelfth hour and the dawn are at hand. Then the goddess of the eleventh hour makes way for the goddess of the twelfth hour, and she calls aloud the name of the Guardian of the gate. Flung wide are the portals, and the Boat of Ra passes through.

"Darkness has fallen, and births shine forth" is the name of the twelfth country of the Duat. On the prow of the Boat is the great scarab of Khepera, ready to make the transformations of Ra ere he reaches the end of the Duat. Not like other lands is this twelfth region of the Duat, for it is enclosed in the body of a vast and monstrous serpent. "Life of the Gods" is his name, and through this great and huge frame travels the Boat of Millions of Years. Twelve of the worshippers of Ra seize the towing-ropes and drag the Boat onward, and here in the body of the serpent is Ra transformed into Khepera and is alive again, for now the journey through the Duat is near the end. Standing by the mouth of the serpent are twelve goddesses; to these the Worshippers of Ra yield the towing-ropes, and they draw the Boat to the eastern horizon of heaven. And now the dead corpse of Ra is cast out of the Boat, as the husk is cast away when the grain is winnowed out, for the soul and the life of Ra are in the scarab of Khepera, and the transformations of Ra are completed. With shouting and singing, with joy and with gladness, the Boat of Ra passes out of the Duat.

Glorious is the Manzet Boat, speeding to the sunrise! Wide, swing wide the portals, and usher in the day. Between the sycamores of turquoise comes the Boat of Ra, and the mountain of Bakhu is flushed with light. The serpent, guardian of the Great Green Waters, beholds Ra in glory in the eastern horizon of heaven, and the rays glitter on his scales.

Glorious is the Manzet Boat, borne upon the river, flashing in the splendour and the light of open day. In the foam at the prow of the Boat sports the Abtu-fish, darting through the gleaming spray, and the Ant-fish is seen in the whirlpool of turquoise. From the earth rises up the sound of rejoicing, for all created things praise Ra at his rising.

Hail to thee, Ra, at thy rising; the night and the darkness are past. At the dawn of the day thou shinest, the heavens are filled with thy light. King of the Gods art thou, all glory and triumph are thine. The Gods come as dogs to thy feet, rejoicing to greet thee at dawn. Hail to thee Ra, at thy rising; at thy coming all men are glad. In joy dost thou come in the morning, with glory thou rulest the world. The stars of the heavens adore thee, the Gods of the earth exalt thee, Lord of the Heavens art thou. Hail to thee, Ra, at thy rising! None can express thy glory, Lord of all Wisdom and Truth. The souls of the East attend thee, the souls of the West are thy servants, the North and the South adore thee. Worshipped art thou, our Ruler, by those whom thou hast created, Thou risest in heaven's horizon, thou causest mankind to rejoice. Hail to thee, Ra, at thy rising; at thy rising in beauty, O Ra.

The Princess and the Demon

Published: Prisse d'Avennes, *Monuments Egyptiens,*
pl. xxiv.
Translated: Wiedemann, *Religion of the Ancient Egyptians,*
p. 275.

This tale is sculptured on a sandstone tablet found by Champollion in the temple of Khonsu at Thebes, and now in the Bibliothèque Nationale at Paris.

There are twenty-eight horizontal lines of inscription, and above them is a scene of two boats of Khonsu borne on the shoulders of priests, with the king offering incense before them.

When first translated, the tale was supposed to be a record of fact, but now it is generally considered a folk-tale, redounding to the credit and glory of Khonsu, and therefore made use of by the priests of that god. The king mentioned in it cannot be identified with any of the historical monarchs of Egypt, although his personal name, Rameses, is sufficiently common among the rulers of the xxth dynasty.

The King's Dream

Published: Lepsius, *Denkmäler,* iii, 68.
Translated: Breasted, *Ancient Records,* ii, 810–815.

The inscription is sculptured on a round-topped stela of red granite, fourteen feet high, set up in the little temple which lies between the paws of the Great Sphinx.

The temple was excavated by Captain Caviglia in 1817. It forms the end of a processional way which leads downwards by paved causeways and flights of steps from the edge of the desert into the sanctuary (see Vyse, *Pyramids of Gizeh*, iii, 107). The tiny shrine is only ten feet long by five wide, and at its farthest end, with its back to the breast of the Sphinx, stands this stela.

The inscription, which is in horizontal lines, is surmounted by a scene, duplicated to right and left, of the king making a libation of water and burning incense before the figure of a Sphinx couchant upon a pylon or altar. The lower half of the stela is so mutilated that the inscription is either destroyed or illegible.

The inscription purports to be of the time of Thothmes IV, a king of the xviiith dynasty, about 1400 B.C.; erected by that monarch as a votive offering. But from the evidence of the language in which the inscription is couched it is obviously much later; Erman dates it to a period between the xxiiird and xxvith dynasties. It may, however, be a restoration of an earlier record, though of the early inscription nothing remains.

The Coming of the Great Queen

Published: Naville, *Deir el Bahari*, ii, pls. xlvi–li (with translation).

Translated: Breasted, *Ancient Records*, ii, 187–220.

The inscription, with the scenes illustrating it, are sculptured on the walls of the temple of Deir el Bahari, on the north side of the retaining wall of the upper platform.

The great building, known in modern times as the temple of Deir el Bahari, was erected by Queen Hatshepsut of the xviiith dynasty, about 1500 B.C., for the double purpose of her own funerary cult, and of the worship of the goddess Hathor. The chief events of the Queen's reign are sculptured on the walls; the record of her divine descent naturally holds a prominent place. The inscriptions in the temple were wrecked and restored anciently, therefore much of the record is lost. Fortunately, however, Amenhotep III, a king of the same dynasty rather more than a century later than Hatshepsut, adorned his temple of Luxor with similar scenes and inscriptions, relating to his own divine descent, changing of course the names of the mother and child and making a few immaterial alterations in the inscriptions. By means of this later example the whole of the earlier record is made clear.

The white colonnades of Hatshepsut's temple, set against a background of dark cliffs, form one of the most striking scenes in the valley of the Nile. The temple was used at one time as a Coptic village; hence its modern name of Deir el Bahari, the Northern Convent.

It has recently been excavated and restored by Dr. Naville for the Egypt Exploration Fund.

The Book of Thoth

Published: Spiegelberg, *Demotische Papyrus* (Cairo Catalogue).
Translated: Petrie, *Egyptian Tales*, ii, 89.

This story is written in demotic on a papyrus found at Thebes in the grave of a Coptic monk. It was among other papyri, written in hieratic and in Coptic, in a wooden chest, and is now in the Cairo Museum. Demotic is the script in which the latest form of the Egyptian language was written; the earliest example remaining is of the reign of Shabaka of the xxvth dynasty, about 715 B.C.; it continued in use till Roman times, when it was superseded by the Greek alphabet.

The papyrus is of the Ptolemaic period, but the exact date is uncertain, as the colophon at the end is partly illegible.

The year 15 only is visible, which, however, is not sufficient guide to the reign of the king under whom it was written.

The legend given in this book is part only of a much longer tale; it is in fact a story within a story, told by the *ka* of Ahura to the high priest of Memphis, when he ventured into the tomb of Nefer-ka-ptah in search of the Book of Thoth.

The Book of Thoth is said to contain only two pages; it must therefore have been a roll of papyrus written on both sides.

Osiris

Original: Plutarch, *De Iside et Osiride*.
Translated: Mead, *Thrice-greatest Hermes,* i, 278.

The treatise on Isis and Osiris was written by Plutarch, himself an initiate into the Osiris-mysteries, to a fellow-initiate, a woman named Klea. It was written at Delphi in the second century A.D.

It is the only connected account remaining of the death of Osiris and the wanderings of Isis. Though of so late a date, it is found to be correct on the whole when checked by the inscriptions and sculpture of Pharaonic times.

The so-called Ritual of Denderah is our principal authority for the worship of Osiris in the chief temples of Egypt on the festivals of the month of Khoiakh. The Ritual is sculptured on the walls of the temple of Denderah, and gives in great detail the rites in use, and even the size and material of the symbolical images. The inscription dates to the Ptolemaic period, but the Ritual is considerably earlier.

"Mystery-plays" of the death of Osiris and of the repulse of Set by Horus appear to have been enacted on certain great occasions at the chief centres of worship. The principal part was that of Horus, which was acted by the Pharaoh himself in the capital, and by the chief local notabilities in provincial centres.

The Scorpions of Isis

Published: Golénischeff, *Metternichstele* (with German translation).
Translated: Budge, *Legends of the Gods,* p. 157.

This inscription is sculptured on a round-topped stela of

serpentine (?), fixed in a square pedestal. It was found at Alexandria at the beginning of the nineteenth century, and was presented to Prince Metternich by Mohamed Ali in 1828.

The front, back, and sides of both stela and pedestal are sculptured with horizontal and vertical lines of inscription and with mythological figures. The stela belongs to a class of amuletic objects, usually called Cippi of Horus, which are inscribed with magical spells against all animals "biting with their mouths or stinging with their tails." This stela is the largest Cippus of Horus known. On the front is sculptured in high relief the figure of Horus represented as a naked child, standing on two crocodiles, and holding a lion, a gazelle, scorpions, and snakes in his hands. He stands within a shrine, which is surmounted by the head of Bes. Isis and Thoth, the goddesses of the South and North, and other mythological figures and emblems are within and without the shrine. Above this scene are horizontal registers filled with figures, possibly representing scenes from legends which are now lost.

The text which preserves the story of the scorpions of Isis is inscribed on the back of the tablet, ll. 48–70. The date of the stela is about 370 B.C., in the reign of Nectanebo I, of the xxxth dynasty.

The Black Pig

Published: Naville, *Das Aegyptische Todtenbuch,* pl. cxxiv. Translated: Budge, *Book of the Dead,* ch. cxii.

The so-called Book of the Dead is a compilation of texts which are found, written on papyri or on coffins, in the tombs. No copy containing all the chapters is known; the order has therefore been arranged from a comparison of many examples.

The ancient name of these texts is "Chapters of Coming forth to the Day"; the modern name is "Book of the Dead," as it is evidently a manual for the use of the dead. It consists of a series of prayers, hymns, magical formulae, and allusions to mythological stories, a knowledge of which was considered necessary in order to escape the perils and dangers of the life hereafter. It is obviously very ancient, for even in the earliest known examples, the Pyramid Texts of the vith dynasty, the text is often very corrupt. The Pyramid Texts show traces of very primitive usages and cults, many of which are lost in the later forms of the Book of the Dead.

The story related under the name of the Black Pig refers to an incident in the war between Horus and Set, and is not known elsewhere. Probably many such legends were current in ancient Egypt, but few have been preserved to us intact. Horus was the great hero-god, and, like the heroes of other countries, he absorbed all the legends of local champions. Some of his exploits and adventures seem to have been so well known that a mere allusion was sufficient to recall them to the mind of the reader. Sometimes a short and, to us, confused account is given, as in chapter cxiii of the Book of the Dead, where the restoration to Horus of his hands and arms, which have been lost in a swamp, is related in a manner which conveys very little to the modern reader.

A great number of legends have been preserved in magical papyri, but even among these the quantity of tantalising allusions is larger than the number of complete legends. Thus, in the Demotic Papyrus of London and Leyden, a charm against fever begins "Horus was going up a hill at midday in the verdure season, mounted on a white horse." He finds the gods eating, and they invite him to join them, but he refuses as he has fever. This is all that is said, but it is evidently an allusion to a well-known story.

The Battles of Horus

Published: Naville, *Mythe d'Horus* (with French translation).

Translated: Wiedemann, *Religion of the Ancient Egyptians,* p. 69.

The account of the war between Horus and Set is sculptured

on the inner part of the west side of the girdle-wall of the temple of Edfu. The whole temple is dedicated to Horus; though undoubtedly an early foundation, the present structure dates only to the Ptolemaic period. It was begun by Ptolemy III Euergetes I, and took 180 years to build and decorate. The girdle-wall, on which these scenes and inscriptions were sculptured, was built and decorated about 100 B.C., either by Soter II or Alexander I.

The temple was excavated by Mariette, and is the most perfect in condition of all the temples in Egypt, for with the exception of the wanton multilation of the faces, probably by Christian fanatics, both building and sculpture are untouched save by time.

The inscription appears to give in legendary form a fairly accurate account of tribal battles of a very early period. Though the actual inscription is of a late date, many primitive ideas are preserved, especially in the hymns of the women to Horus. "Eat ye the flesh of the vanquished, drink ye his blood," is not a sentiment of the civilisation of Ptolemaic times. Human sacrifice, however, appears to have been practised in Egypt at all periods. Harvest victims were burnt at Eleithyapolis (El Kab). Amasis II of the xxvith dynasty put an end to human sacrifice at Heliopolis; Diodorus says that red-haired men were offered up at the sepulchre of Osiris; as the king was the incarnate Osiris, this would mean that human sacrifices were made at the royal graves, probably during the funeral ceremonies. The Book of the Dead also continually alludes to human sacrifice. At Edfu an altar was found sculptured with representations of offerings in which human beings are the victims. Small figures, carved in the round, are known, which are in the form of bound captives; and show probably the method of binding the victim; the legs are bent at the knees, and the feet bound to the thighs; the arms are bent at the elbows and securely lashed to the body. This is not the ordinary way of binding a prisoner, but is a special method reserved probably for a human victim. The figures represent sometimes men, sometimes women.

Judging by the representations and scenes of the girdle-wall, a "mystery-play" was acted in the temple of Edfu, the Pharaoh

Egyptian name, but is now called the Book of Gates, for in it the gates are more important than the countries which they divide. (For a comparison of the two books, see Budge, *Egyptian Heaven and Hell*). The Book of Gates is rarer than the Book of Am Duat, and is found sculptured on sarcophagi; the finest example being the alabaster sarcophagus of Seti I, now in the Soane Museum in London.

The Book of Am Duat is found both in papyri and on tomb-walls, the earliest example of the latter being the tomb of Amenhotep II of the xviiith dynasty. It is a compilation by the theologians of that period; an attempt to combine into one homogeneous whole several distinct ideas of the next world and the life hereafter. The fourth and fifth countries of the Duat are obviously one complete kingdom, ruled by the god Sokar, the Memphite god of the dead. As Memphis was a very important religious centre, its god of the dead and his kingdom had to be included in the Duat of Ra, in spite of the fact that it was a waterless desert, and that it ended with the Morning Star. It was a region totally different from any other kingdom of the here-after; no river ran through it; it was inhabited by neither gods nor spirits, but by enormous and horrible reptiles. The ingenu-ity of the compilers of this Book in turning the Book of Ra into a serpent, which could dispense with the river and glide over the sand, is certainly remarkable.

Another Morning Star appears also in the tenth hour, and the breeze of morning seems to be felt by the goddesses in the eleventh hour, for they raise their hands to shelter their faces from it. Budge (*Egyptian Heaven and Hell*) suggests also that the Egyptians looked upon the red clouds of the dawn as being tinged with the reflection from the pits of flame. These indica-tions of morning appearing in the wrong place point clearly to the fact of the book being a compilation, more or less clumsy.

The first hour seems to have been added in order to make a good introduction to the compilation. The last hour is evidently a compromise. The most ancient idea with regard to the sunrise was that the Sun was born anew every morning of the Sky-goddess Nut. This theory does not fit with the dogma of the Sun's nightly journey through the Other World in a Boat;

therefore the last hour is represented as a dark and tortuous passage symbolising the womb of the goddess. The birth of the Sun was the most important event of the day to his worshippers, consequently the account of the last hour is found frequently on papyri, buried in the graves.

The Duat, or Other World, was generally supposed to be the region lying to the north of Egypt; the delta by the Egyptians of the South; the Mediterranean and its islands by the delta-people.

The Egyptians had an abridgment or summary of this long account of Ra's night-journey. It was always written on papyrus in vertical columns, with all the scenes and long speeches omitted. It gives the name of each gate and country and of the goddess of every hour; sometimes, though not always, the names of the gods who live in the different regions; and always the magical words of Ra to the inhabitants of each land. Felicitous results here and hereafter are promised to all who know the words and scenes thoroughly.

The hymn to Ra is a paraphrase of hymns which are still extant.

List of Gods Mentioned

Abtu-fish.—A mythological fish which accompanies the Boat of Ra at sunrise.

Amemt.—The mythical animal which devours the hearts of the wicked at the Judgment of Osiris.

Amon.—God of Thebes. In and after the xviiith dynasty he became the supreme deity of Egypt under the name of Amon-Ra.

Ant-fish.—A mythological fish which accompanies the Boat of Ra at sunrise.

Anubis.—A jackal-headed deity who presided over the embalming of the dead. He was said to be the illegitimate son of Osiris and Nephthys, and, in the form of a dog, to have protected Isis in her wanderings.

Apep.—The enemy of Ra in the Duat.

Astarte.—A Syrian goddess, whose name is found occasionally in Egyptian inscriptions.

Atmu.—An early name of the solar deity worshipped at Heliopolis. In later times, the name of the setting sun.

Bes.—A bandy-legged dwarf with horns. God of music and pleasure, and protector of children. Possibly also a god of birth.

Besa.—A spirit of the corn.

Geb.—The earth-god, father of Osiris.

Harmakhis.—Horus on the Horizon, i.e. the sun at its rising and setting.

Harpocrates.—Horus the Child, son of Isis and Osiris.

Hathor.—Goddess of love and beauty; often identified with all the other goddesses, including Sekhmet.

Hekt.—The frog-headed goddess of birth.

Her-desuf.—A form of Horus.

Horakhti.—The Horizon-Horus. The same as Harmakhis.

Horus.—The hawk-headed god is, properly speaking, the brother of Isis and Osiris; but is constantly confused with Horus the Child, and is called Avenger or Protector of his Father.

73

Isis.—The greatest of Egyptian goddesses, wife of Osiris, and mother of Harpocrates.

Khepera.—The rising sun, god of resurrection.

Khnum.—The ram-headed god of the cataract, who creates man upon the potter's wheel.

Khonsu.—The moon-god at Thebes.

Mehen.—The serpent who protects Ra in the Duat.

Mentu.—God of war.

Meskhent.—Goddess of birth.

Min.—Father of gods and men. God of Koptos.

Neith.—Goddess of Saïs. Identified by the Greeks with Athena.

Nekhbet.—The vulture-goddess of Upper Egypt.

Nephthys.—Sister of Isis and Osiris.

Nepra.—A spirit of the corn.

Nun.—God of the primaeval waters.

Nut.—The sky-goddess, mother of Osiris.

Osiris.—One of the chief gods of Egypt. Murdered and torn to pieces by his brother Set, re-vivified by Isis and Horus.

Ra.—The Sun-god, one of the chief gods of Egypt. Heliopolis (the On of the Bible) was the principal centre of his worship.

Sekhmet.—The lioness-headed goddess of Memphis.

Selk.—The scorpion-goddess.

Set.—Brother and murderer of Osiris. Looked upon, in late times, as the Author of Evil.

Shu.—Twin-brother of Tefnut. He holds up the sky above the earth.

Sokar.—The hawk-headed god of the dead. When fused with Ptah (Ptah-Sokar) he appears in the form of a misshapen dwarf, and is then looked upon as a god of resurrection.

Tatanen.—An obscure god, generally fused with Ptah of Memphis as Ptah-Tatanen.

Ta-urt.—The hippopotamus goddess of birth.

Tefnut.—Lioness-headed. Twin-sister of Shu. The two form the constellation Gemini.

Tepu-yn.—A spirit of the corn.

Thoth.—The ibis-headed god of all learning and magic. Chief centre of worship Khemennu or Hermopolis, now called Eshmunen.

Uazet.—Goddess of Lower Egypt.

Up-uaut.—The jackal-god of Siut.